RESTLESS
TILL WE REST
IN YOU

The Saints Speak Today Series

Restless Till We Rest in You

60 Reflections From the Writings of
St. Augustine

COMPILED BY
PAUL THIGPEN

CHARIS
SERVANT PUBLICATIONS
ANN ARBOR, MICHIGAN

Charis Books is an imprint of Servant Publications especially designed to serve Roman Catholics.

Servant Publications
P.O. Box 8617
Ann Arbor, MI 48107

Cover design: Left Coast Design, Portland, OR

98 99 00 10 9 8 7 6 5 4 3 2 1

Printed in the United States of America
ISBN 1-56955-034-4

Library of Congress Cataloging-in-Publication Data on file.

CONTENTS

"Prepare a Place for Love ..." Learn First to Fear God

"For Now, We Are Still Fighting ..." The Struggle for Holiness

"He Is the One I Seek ..."
God's Word and Sacraments Deepen Our Faith

INTRODUCTION

Augustine:
Saint of the Restless Heart

The times were restless.

The western provinces of the Roman Empire were a cauldron of political intrigue in the days of St. Augustine, during the late fourth and early fifth centuries. Rome's age-long supremacy was crumbling. Military and bureaucratic leadership found themselves in turmoil over inner contests for power and prestige, with the consequent turnover sometimes reaching to the throne of the emperor himself. In North Africa, where St. Augustine spent most of his days, mercenary generals itching to become something greater followed the example of their European counterparts, revolting and setting up fiefdoms in defiance of imperial control.

The restlessness of the barbarian tribes, seeking new areas for settlement, had not waned with their earlier conquests beyond the imperial borders. The Ostrogoths roved through Italy, while the Visigoths sacked Rome and swarmed through Spain like locusts. The Vandals, displacing waves of refugees before them, poured from Gaul into Spain and finally across the Straits of Gibraltar, eighty thousand strong, flooding North Africa and devastating the land. Roman settlements that they attacked on the African coast were already weary from the vexing raids they had long suffered from the seminomadic peoples of the interior.

The Church could find no more rest than could the empire. Diocletian's persecutions were now only a sorrowful memory, but a still-sizeable pagan population blamed the empire's woes on the new religion of the Nazarene. Manichaean preachers had wandered from the mysterious East into the declining cities of the West, unsettling Christians and pagans alike with their dark and curious doctrines of two gods, strange prophets, and a secret wisdom.

Arius, the popular African priest, had been condemned by an ecumenical Church council for denying that Christ was fully God; yet he had gained a feverish following within the Christian community—including bishops, emperors, and thousands of the barbarian invaders. The Pelagian heresies also emerged to trouble the ecclesiastical waters, from Britain all the way to Bethlehem. In North Africa, the Church was rattled further by the Donatist schism: Christians of rigorous standards were pitted violently against those who were more lax, with ethnic and regional jealousies intensifying the agitations to the point of riots, terrorist attacks, and government reprisals.

In the midst of this social, political, and spiritual chaos walked a man whose personal journey reflected the restlessness of his surroundings. Born in 354 in Thagaste, North Africa, St. Augustine moved back and forth between that little town and the bustling port of Carthage. He later settled in Rome, then farther north at Milan, before finally returning to North Africa. During these wanderings, his career drifted from the rhetorician's classroom to the imperial court's halls to the philosopher's colony, and finally on to the priest's altar and the bishop's chair.

Equally restless was his spiritual quest. The son of a Christian mother and a pagan father, in his childhood Augustine had sided first with her and then with his father, and then as a youth he was seduced by the exotic tales of the Manichees. When their teachings left him intellectually unsatisfied, however, he turned to the books of the Neo-Platonic philosophers. Though he felt nourished by these more heady volumes, he nevertheless found their truths incomplete. Only in the humble yet profound Christian Scriptures, the elegant, convicting preaching of St. Ambrose, and the stubborn, matured devotion of his mother did he finally discover a faith he could embrace without reservation.

Yet even then St. Augustine's restlessness was far from over, for—in the words of the scriptural text he once quoted wearily when emerging from his study—"When a man is finished, he is just beginning" (Sirach 18:7). He eventually settled permanently, though reluctantly, in Hippo, however, where he was ordained in 391 and consecrated bishop in 395. He remained fixed as well in his Catholic faith and remained a fiercely orthodox leader up to his death in 430. Yet the mind and the heart of this remarkable saint were far from settled; for him, the end of one pursuit was merely the start of another. Like a lion intent on his prey, the bishop's soul continued to roam the earth: bounding up mystical heights, leaping into intellectual depths, braving historical currents, searching out the caves and crevices of private memory and experience, all to hunt down the spiritual truths for which he maintained such a ravenous appetite.

St. Augustine's quarry was stunning in its variety and abundance. In *The Confessions* (c. 397), perhaps his most famous work, he captured the very essence of the Christian life of prayer, praise, and passion, while creating a timeless model of painfully honest, thoroughly intriguing autobiography. His celebrated *City of God* (413-26) was prompted by the fall of Rome, a catastrophe that sent shock waves throughout the Mediterranean world and called into question for his trembling contemporaries all earthly foundations for social and political stability. This hefty text, comprising twenty-two volumes, exerted enormous influence on Western thought for the next thousand years and beyond by offering a theology of history—a profound vision of time and eternity that Thomas Merton has wisely called "the autobiography of the Catholic Church."

Beginning in his early days, St. Augustine composed a number of philosophical works, but his speculative thought climbed to unequaled heights in his treatise *On the Trinity* (419). The Manichees, Pelagians, Donatists, and other controversialists of the day provoked him to produce a number of polemical works addressing issues that today still engage Christians in debate. He viewed teaching the Scriptures to his flock as the heart of his work as a bishop: In his treatise *On Christian Doctrine* (396, 427) he laid out the principles for examining biblical texts, which he taught by example in his numerous homilies and scriptural expositions. The great themes of these pastoral labors are summarized in his mature doctrinal writings, most notably his handbook of the Christian life, the *Enchiridion on Faith, Hope and Love* (421).

Thus, St. Augustine has filled our spiritual table with choice meats of every description, and he bids us come and dine. No doubt entire lifetimes could be spent, and have been spent, trying to digest so massive a feast. Yet even those of us who can only sample the offerings must be grateful that one of the most brilliant, most passionate, most ferocious minds in the history of the Church gave himself so relentlessly to a lifelong spiritual hunt in order to bring back to us such bountiful game.

The primary sources for this particular collection of the saint's thoughts are by no means representative of the entire corpus of his work, nor perhaps could they have been, given the immensity of that corpus. Not surprisingly, the majority of the excerpts here come from *The Confessions:* After all, a new book of devotional readings, Scripture texts, and prayers could hardly have passed by this most exquisite of all devotional narrations, itself steeped in the language of Scripture and uttered in the form of a book-length prayer.

The rich and complex thought of St. Augustine's philosophical, polemical, and doctrinal treatises is much more difficult to present meaningfully in small installments. Therefore, aside from a few shining pearls from *The City of God*, most of the other passages here have come from his homilies.

Despite his rare genius and intimidating erudition, when he preached to the common people St. Augustine had the charming ability to express even the most difficult, abstract principles in practical, concrete forms. Drawing from his native African tradition of witty, colorful language, he became a master of the vivid image, the telling detail, the apt metaphor, the illuminating analogy. All these he often combined to spin out persuasive parables, as his Lord had done centuries before him.

The bishop's audiences delighted in what they heard. They often interrupted his sermons with cries of admiration and waves of applause. In reading his words, we may well at times feel compelled to do the same.

Most of the homily excerpts here have come from sermons on the Gospel of St. John and the Epistles of St. John. And so they should: St. Augustine had a special attachment to the Johannine literature, not least of all because of its emphasis on love—which, as he never tired of telling his listeners, is the sum and summit of the Christian life. Meditating on the epistles especially, St. Augustine found in these texts a cure for countless spiritual ailments: anger and bitterness, pride and vainglory, greed and selfishness, indifference and complacency.

At the same time, St. John's words breathe a spirit that the bishop found akin to his own—now lofty and philosophical, now intimate and passionate. Reading the soaring speculations and bittersweet sighs of *The Confessions*, we are left with no doubt that its author envied both of that apostle's characteristic postures: For St. John was known to spread his wings on the heights of heavenly perspective, like the eagle that is his ancient symbol; but he was also known as the one who leaned on the breast of Jesus, enjoying the precious rest that St. Augustine longed for but found so elusive.

Some day, the good bishop reminded himself again and again, he, too, would look down from those glorious heights even while he reclined in the very bosom of the Lord. The heavenly Jerusalem, the homeland for which he pined, was also the place of promised rest, the site of the eternal Sabbath that awaits the people of God. The day would come when faith would become sight, when desire would be swallowed up in delight, when the things that could be shaken would be shaken off forever, and when all that remained would be the One who remains forever. Nothing less, Augustine insisted, was worth living for.

Until that final eternal day, however, there was much for a bishop to do in such unsettled times. Until the Sabbath rest should come, his restlessness would never cease, and he would run from challenge to challenge, from need to need, scattering his ample gifts in every direction.

Did the pagan philosophers offer a useful insight? He must sharpen it on the whetting stone of Scripture and make it a tool for his theology. Did the heretics cast a doctrinal stone through the open door of the Church? He must take it up, sculpt it according to Catholic truth, and toss it back to them. Did he remember an act of petty vandalism he had committed as a child? He must rend the fabric of that memory, drawing out its threads to begin weaving a Christian psychology. Did he see a lizard lazing in the sun? He must peer at the rock beneath it to find a moral lesson.

From such perpetual restlessness his heirs in the faith have profited sweetly. He was a tireless spiritual winemaker: driven to pluck every little experience, every passing event or nearby object, and to squeeze from them every last drop of vital juice, so he could pour it in the cask of his superb mind, ferment it in the deep cellar of his soul, and offer in due time the intoxicating wine of a godly wisdom. In this book, modest vessel that it is, are offered a few sips that should send readers looking for a longer, deeper draft.

Even so, we must never forget that for St. Augustine, the wine was meant to be an elixir of love. He himself was inebriated with the love of the One who had paid so dearly to redeem him. Never did he lose sight of the fact that the Truth for which he hungered so sharply was a Person; that Wisdom himself had come from heaven to rescue us, remake us, and claim us for his own.

If we would be not only St. Augustine's disciples but also his friends, we must listen carefully to his instructions about how friends are to be loved: "In God, then, let your friends be loved; and draw to him along with you as many souls as you can. Say to them: 'He is the One we should love. He is the One. He has created the world, and he is not far from us. For when he created the world, he did not abandon it. All that exists comes from him and is in him.'"[1]

This is the heart of what St. Augustine has to tell us; and if his words succeed in drawing us to the Lord then he has been to us the best of friends.

Meanwhile, the times are again restless. Social, political, and spiritual chaos threaten to engulf us today even as it threatened St. Augustine and his flock. The good bishop died as the brutal Vandals marched toward Hippo, bringing to an end the world as he had known it; do we have any assurances that our world, too, is not, even now, passing away into the night? Worse yet, today the barbarians are not at the gates; they are within the gates, for we have reared them ourselves.

If St. Augustine could speak today, surely his counsel would be the same as that he gave his contemporaries: Let the wickedness around you and within you drive you to the mercy of God. Let the loss of all that fades and decays wean you from the fickle love of a fleeting world. He is the One we should love. He is our eternal Sabbath, our place of final repose.

The opening prayer of *The Confessions* still rings clearly above the din of a disordered world: "You have made us for yourself, Lord, and our hearts are restless till they find their rest in you."[2]

"Strength of My Soul ..."

All We Need We Find in God

DAY 1
We Will Never Rest
Until We Find Our Rest in God

Only in God is my soul at rest; from him comes my salvation. He only is my rock and my stronghold: I shall not be disturbed at all.

PSALM 62:2-3, NAB

MORNING READING

"You are great, Lord, and greatly to be praised; your power is great, and your wisdom is infinite" [see Ps 145:3]. Man desires to praise you, Lord, for he is one of your creatures. Though he bears the mark of death wherever he goes as a testimony to his sin—a reminder that you resist the proud—yet still, because man is a part of your creation, he desires to praise you. You move us to delight in praising you, for you have made us for yourself, and our hearts are restless till they find their rest in you.

No being can be at the same time opposed to God and in harmony with itself.

ST. BERNARD OF CLAIRVAUX

FOR REFLECTION

Lord, help me give up my all my frenzied pursuits to lay my head on your breast and to be quieted there like a little child.

EVENING READING

What tortuous ways I walked! Woe to that rash soul of mine, that hoped by abandoning you, Lord, to find something better! It tossed and turned, upon its back, upon its sides, upon its belly, yet it found every place it lay to be hard—you alone are my rest. And behold, you are near at hand, and you deliver us from our wretched wanderings, and you settle us in your own way. And you comfort us, saying: "Run, I will carry you; yes, I will lead you to the end of your journey, and there also I will carry you."

DAY 2
God's Nature Is a Marvelous Mystery

Can you penetrate the designs of God? Dare you vie with the perfection of the Almighty?

JOB 11:7, NAB

MORNING READING

For who is Lord but our Lord? Or who is God besides our God? Most high, most excellent, most mighty, most omnipotent; most merciful and most just; most hidden and most near; most beautiful and most strong; constant, yet incomprehensible; unchangeable, yet changing all things; never new, never old; renewing all things, yet bringing old age upon the proud, without their knowing it; always working, yet always at rest; gathering, yet needing nothing; upholding, filling and protecting; creating, nourishing and perfecting; still seeking, though you lack nothing. You love, but are not agitated by your love; you are jealous, yet free from care, you are angry, yet you remain tranquil.

To speak of the Godhead is, I know, like trying to cross the ocean on a raft, or trying to fly to the stars on a little bird's wings.

ST. GREGORY NAZIANZEN

FOR REFLECTION

My God, even my wildest imaginations can only guess at the mysteries of your infinity, your eternity, your richness, your perfection!

EVENING READING

Lord, you change your works, but not your plans. You embrace what you find, without ever having truly lost. You are never in need, yet you rejoice in what you gain; never greedy, yet you demand a profit. Men give to you more than is required, hoping to put you in their debt; yet who has anything to give that isn't already yours? You pay us as if in debt to us, yet you owe us nothing; and when you forgive debts, you lose nothing. Yet, my God, my life, my holy Joy, is all this I have said enough? Can anyone who speaks of you ever say enough?

True Joy Is Found Only in God

Rejoice in the Lord always; again I will say, Rejoice.

PHILIPPIANS 4:4

MORNING READING

Let it be far from me to think myself happy because of any joy I may have now, whatever joy it may be. For there is a joy not granted to the wicked, but only to those who worship you thankfully—and you are yourself this joy. This is the happy life: to rejoice to you, in you, and for you. This is it and there is no other. Those who think there is another kind of joy pursue happiness elsewhere, but theirs is not a true joy. The only true happiness is to rejoice in you.

Fully to enjoy is to glorify. In commanding us to glorify him, God is inviting us to enjoy him.

C.S. LEWIS

FOR REFLECTION

To see you, Lord, is to know you; to know you is to love you; to love you is to enjoy you—so show yourself to me, and my joy will be complete!

EVENING READING

Because God is all our joy, whoever wants to rejoice securely should rejoice in him, who cannot perish. For why, my brothers and sisters, would you rejoice in silver? Either your silver will perish, or you will, and no one knows which will perish first. Only one thing is certain: Both shall perish. What is uncertain is which one will perish first. For neither can you remain here always, nor can silver remain here always; so also with gold, wardrobes, houses, money, real estate—and in the end, even the light by which we enjoy all these things. So do not be willing, then, to rejoice in such things as these. Rejoice instead in the light that has no setting; rejoice in the dawn which no yesterday precedes, and no tomorrow follows.

DAY 4
Without God, We Have Nothing and We Are Nothing

What is man, that you should be mindful of him, or the son of man, that you should care for him?

PSALM 8:5, NAB

MORNING READING

Give yourself to me, my God; restore yourself to me. Behold, I love you; and if my love be too little, let me love you even more strongly. I am unable to measure my love in order to know how much there is still lacking in me before my life can run into your embrace and not be turned away, until my life is hidden in the secret place of your presence. This only I know: that woe is me if I am not in you—not only in my outward life, but also deep within myself—and all the abundance I have that is not my God is only poverty.

God thirsts for you, not because you are his waters of everlasting life, but because you are the thirst, he the waters. He needs you only because you need him. Without him you are imperfect; but without you he is perfect. It is the echo that needs the Voice, and not the Voice that needs the echo.

ARCHBISHOP FULTON J. SHEEN

FOR REFLECTION

Lord, if I have everything but you, I have nothing; and if I have you and nothing else, I have everything.

EVENING READING

Before I was, Lord, you were; nor was I anything at all that you should grant me the gift of existence. And yet, see how I exist now simply because of your goodness, which has made provision for all that you have made me to be and all that you made me from. For you had no need of me, nor could I be of any use to you, my Lord and my God. It is not as if I am of such assistance to you with my service, that I could keep you from tiring in your work, or that your power would be any less without my help. Nor is it as if you were a field that I cultivate, so that you would go untended if I did not tend you. Instead, you have made me so that I may worship and serve you, so that good may come to me from you—for you are the One who has made me capable of receiving what is good.

When We Seek to Fulfill Our Desires Apart From God, We Mistakenly Seek What Is Found Perfectly Only in God

Do not be deceived, my beloved brethren. Every good endowment and every perfect gift is from above, coming down from the Father of lights with whom there is no variation or shadow due to change.

JAMES 1:16-17

MORNING READING

Now there is an attractiveness in all beautiful bodies, and in gold and silver and all things. The touch of flesh has its own power to please, and each of the other senses have their proper objects in physical sensations. Worldly honor also has its own glory, and the power to command and to overcome. And yet, to acquire all these pleasures, we must not depart from you, Lord, or deviate from your law. Human friendships are also endeared by a sweet bond, joining many souls together as one. Yet because of these and similar things, good in themselves, sin is committed—because we have an inordinate preference for these good things of a lower order, and we neglect the better and higher good. We neglect You, Lord God, your truth and your law. For all these lesser good things have their delights, but nothing like my Lord God, who has created all things.

Hope always draws the soul from the beauty that is seen to what is beyond, always kindles the desire for the hidden through what is perceived.

St. Gregory of Nyssa

FOR REFLECTION

Fountain of all I desire, everything my heart has ever truly longed for springs from you.

EVENING READING

If physical things please you, praise God for them, but turn back your love to their Creator, so that you may not displease him in the things that please you. The good things that you love are from him, and to the extent that they are used for him, they will remain both good and pleasant. But the things that come from him will be rightly turned into bitterness if they are not rightly loved—if God is forsaken because of a greater love for what he has created.

DAY 6
God Pursues Us So That We May Know Him As He Knows Us

For now we see in a mirror dimly, but then face to face. Now I know in part; then I shall understand fully, even as I have been fully understood.

1 CORINTHIANS 13:12

MORNING READING

Too late have I come to love you, Beauty so ancient, so new! Yes, too late have I come to love you! You were within me, yet I was looking for you outside myself. I, in my ugliness, rushed headlong into the things of beauty you had made. You were with me, but I was not with you. The things you had created kept me far from you; yet if they had not been in you, they would not have been at all. You called to me and cried aloud, and you broke through my deafness. You flashed, and shone, and chased away my blindness. You breathed upon me fragrantly; I drew in my breath, and now I pant for you. I tasted, and now I hunger and thirst for you. You touched me, and I burned to enjoy your peace.

He longs to be in you. He wants his breath to be your breath, his heart in your heart, and his soul in your soul.

ST. JOHN EUDES

FOR REFLECTION

More than my labors, more than my praise, you want me, for my own sake, Jesus; teach me to seek you, too, for your own sake, for you yourself are the reward of my labors and my praise.

EVENING READING

Let me know you, you who know me; let me know you as I am known. Strength of my soul, enter into it, and prepare it for yourself, so that you may have and hold it, without spot or wrinkle. This is my hope, and this is the reason for my rejoicing whenever I rejoice aright. But now, because my misery testifies that I am dissatisfied with myself, you shine forth to me, and satisfy me. You are the object of my love and my desire, so that I blush for myself, and renounce myself, and choose you—for I can please neither you nor myself except in you.

"The One Who Is Our Very Life ..."

Christ Is the Beginning and the End

DAY 7

God Invaded Our World to Defeat Death and to Win Us for Himself

I came that they may have life, and have it abundantly.

JOHN 10:10

MORNING READING

The One who is our very Life descended into our world, and bore our death, and slew it with the abundance of his own life. Thundering, he called out to us to return to him in heaven—to that unseen place from which he had come forth to us. He came first into the Virgin's womb, where the human nature he had created, our mortal flesh, was married to him, so that it might not be mortal forever. From there he appeared "as a bridegroom coming out of his chamber, rejoicing as a strong man to run a race" [see Ps 19:5]. For he did not delay, but ran crying out by his words and deeds, by his death and risen life, by his descent to the grave and ascension into heaven. In all these ways he cried aloud to us to return to him.

Eternal Beauty!... You act as if you could not live without your creature, even though you are Life itself, and everything has its life from you and nothing can live without you. Why then are you so mad? Because you have fallen madly in love with what you have made!

ST. CATHERINE OF SIENA

FOR REFLECTION

Your death for my life—could there be, my Jesus, an exchange any more merciful, any more gracious than that? Seeing you die so that I can live, how can I turn away from so passionate a love?

EVENING READING

When the Lord ascended into heaven, he departed from our sight, so that we might return to our own hearts and find him there. For he left us, and behold, he is here. He could not be with us long, yet he never left us. He went back to heaven, to the place where he had never left, because "the world was made by him" [see Jn 1:10]. And in this world he was, and into this world he came, to save sinners. To him my soul confesses, that he may heal it, for it has sinned against him. Sons of men, how long will you be so slow of heart? Now that Life himself has descended to you, won't you ascend and live?

Christ Descended Into Our Lives So That We Might Someday Ascend Into His

We were buried therefore with him by baptism into death, so that as Christ was raised from the dead by the glory of the Father, we too might walk in newness of life.

ROMANS 6:4

MORNING READING

Would you prefer to love the things of time, and thus pass away with time, or to "love not the world" [see 1 Jn 2:15], and live for eternity with God? The river of temporal things hurries us along, but our Lord Jesus Christ is like a tree sprung up beside the river. He became flesh, died, rose again, and ascended into heaven. He willed to plant himself, as it were, beside the river of the things of time. Are you rushing down the stream to the rapids? Hold fast to the tree. Is love of the world whirling you on? Hold fast to Christ. For you he entered time, so that you might become eternal.

God descends to reascend. He comes down; down from the heights of absolute being into time and space, down into humanity ... down into the very roots and sea-bed of the Nature he had created. But he goes down to come up again and bring the whole ruined world with him.

C.S. LEWIS

FOR REFLECTION

I will hold fast to you, Lord, as you hold fast to me, and you will lift me up from the ruins of my own life into the glory of yours.

EVENING READING

What a great difference there is between two people in prison when one is a criminal and one is a visitor! Sometimes a person comes to visit his friend and enters the prison to visit him. Both are seen to be in prison, but their situations are quite distinct. One is held fast by his condition; the other is brought there by human compassion. In the same way, we were held fast in our mortal state by our guilt, yet Christ in his mercy came down. He came to us captives as a Redeemer, not an oppressor. The Lord shed his blood for us, redeemed us, gave us new hope. As yet our bodies still bear mortality, and we must take his word that our future holds immortality. Yet even while we are being tossed about by the waves on the sea, we have the anchor of hope already fixed upon the land.

DAY 9

Christ Jesus Humbled Himself
to Reconcile Us to God

[Christ] emptied himself, taking the form of a servant, being born in the likeness of men. And being found in human form he humbled himself and became obedient unto death, even death on a cross.

PHILIPPIANS 2:7-8

MORNING READING

Through pride they were unwilling to humble themselves to Christ, the author of humility, and the restrainer of those who swell with pride—to God the Physician, who, being God, for this reason became human, so that humanity might know itself to be merely human. What a mighty remedy! If this remedy will not cure pride, what can? He is God, and he is human; he lays aside his divinity, he hides what is his own by nature, and appears to us in the human nature he had taken to himself. Being God he is made human; yet humanity itself will not acknowledge itself to be human, that is, will not acknowledge itself to be mortal, or frail, or sinful, or sick. If it did, it would at least seek the Physician; but what is more dangerous still, humanity fancies itself to be healthy.

As a ship cannot be built without nails, so a person cannot be saved without humility.

ABBA SYNCLETICE

FOR REFLECTION

In you, Jesus, God himself stooped to wash our feet; serving you, could I dare to lift my heart in pride?

EVENING READING

I was not yet humble enough to grasp the humble Lord Jesus; nor did I yet know what lesson his weakness was meant to teach us. For your Word, the eternal Truth, being so highly exalted above the highest of your creatures, lifts up to himself those who were cast down. But here below he built for himself a lowly cottage of our clay, that he might pull down from their proud heights and win over to himself those he is to make subject to himself. He deflates the swelling of their pride and fosters their love, so that they might go on no further in self-confidence, but rather become weak—just as they see at their feet the Deity himself, weak as he shares our coats of skin.

Jesus, the God-Man, Has Joined Our Human Nature With His Divine Nature to Become the True Mediator

For there is one God, and there is one mediator between God and men, the man Christ Jesus, who gave himself as a ransom for all.

1 TIMOTHY 2:5-6

MORNING READING

The true Mediator, who in your secret mercy you have revealed to the humble, Lord—and have sent him to them so that through him they might also learn humility—that "Mediator between God and humanity, the man Jesus Christ," appeared in order to take his place between mortal sinners and the immortal righteous One. He was mortal as we are mortal; he was righteous as God is righteous. And because the reward of righteousness is life and peace, he was able, through his righteousness united with God, to cancel the death of the sinners he justified—a death he was willing to suffer with them.

Look [God says] at the bridge of my only-begotten Son.... It stretches from heaven to earth, joining the earth of your humanity with the greatness of the Godhead.... So my height bent down to the earth of your humanity, bridging the chasm between us and rebuilding the road.

ST. CATHERINE OF SIENA

FOR REFLECTION

In you, Jesus, the Fire on the mountain of Sinai became the Face on the hill of Calvary; the Light that blinded is now the Light that beckons; and the God we could never have touched has himself grasped us with a nail-scarred hand.

EVENING READING

How you have loved us, good Father, who did not spare your only Son, but delivered him up for us wicked ones! How you have loved us, the ones for whom he, who did not count it robbery to be equal with you, "became obedient to death, even the death of the cross" [see Phil 2:8]. He alone was free among the dead: free to lay down his life and to take it up again. For us he became to you both Victor and Victim—a Victor because he was the Victim. For he was to you both Priest and Sacrifice, and he was a Priest because he was the Sacrifice. Though we were servants, he made children of us, because he was your child and our servant. Rightly, then, is my hope firmly fixed on him.

DAY 11
Christ Himself Is Our Destination; We Must Not Settle for Less

For his sake I have suffered the loss of all things, and count them as refuse, in order that I may gain Christ.... Forgetting what lies behind and straining forward to what lies ahead, I press on toward the goal for the prize of the upward call of God in Christ Jesus.

PHILIPPIANS 3:8, 13, 14

MORNING READING

Though Christ called himself the "Way" [see Jn 14:6], in another sense he is our End. Do not settle down somewhere on the way so that you never come to the End. Whatever else you come to on life's journey, pass on by it, until you come to the End. Some seek money: Do not let it be your end; pass on by, like a traveler in a foreign land. For if you love money, you will be entangled by greed, and greed will be chains on your feet. You will not be able to make any more progress along the way. You seek bodily health, but still do not stop there. For what kind of end is this, which death brings to an end itself, which sickness weakens—a feeble, mortal, fleeting thing? You may of course seek good health so that ill health will not keep you from good works. But for that very reason, we can see that good health itself is not the end, because it is sought for the sake of something else.

Cupidity ... takes created things for ends in themselves, which they are not. The will that seeks rest in creatures for their own sake stops on the way to its true end, terminates in a value which does not exist, and thus frustrates all its deepest capacities for happiness and peace.

THOMAS MERTON

FOR REFLECTION

The Wise Men would have been fools instead to think their journey was ended before they found you, Jesus; and I too must never settle down along the road as long as the star remains over Bethlehem.

EVENING READING

You seek honors; perhaps you seek them in order to accomplish something that pleases God. If so, do not love the honor itself, or you might stop there. Do you seek praise? If you seek God's praise, then you do well. If you seek your own, then not—you are stopping short along the way. See, brothers and sisters, how many things we pass on life's journey that are not the end. These we make use of along the road, taking a break, then traveling on.

"This World's Empty Deceits ..."

Love God Above All Things

The Beauty in the World Around Us Should Draw Us to Its Maker

The heavens are telling the glory of God; and the firmament proclaims his handiwork.... Their voice goes out through all the earth, and their words to the end of the world.

PSALM 19:1, 4

MORNING READING

Look around at the heavens and the earth. They cry out that they were made by Someone else, for they are subject to change and variation, and whatever is self-existent cannot change. Thus heaven and earth proclaim that they did not make themselves: "We exist," they say, "because we have been made; how could we have made ourselves? To do that, we would have had to exist before we existed!" And the simple fact of their existence is the voice with which they speak this truth. But you, Lord, did make these things. You are beautiful, and so they are beautiful; you are good, and so they are good. Because you are, they are. Yet they are not as beautiful or as good or as real as you, their Creator. Compared with you, they are neither beautiful nor good nor even real.

Blessed is the mind that, passing by all creatures, constantly rejoices in God's beauty.

ST. MAXIMUS THE CONFESSOR

FOR REFLECTION

Lord, we are so enthralled by the song that we have forgotten the Singer; teach us to follow the melody back to the Heart that gave it birth.

EVENING READING

The eyes delight in fair and varied forms, and in bright and pleasing colors. Do not allow these to take possession of my soul! Rather let God possess it, the One who made all these things very good indeed. For he is my good—not these other things. That queen of colors, the daylight, floods all that I look upon, wherever I am during the day, gliding past me in manifold forms, soothing me even when I am busy with other things, not noticing it. But this earthly light seasons life for those who love her blindly, giving the world a tempting and fatal sweetness. Yet those who know how to praise you, God, Creator of all, sing you a hymn of praise for such beauty; they are not beguiled by it.

We Must Not Love the Creatures So That We Turn Our Backs on the Creator

Adulterers! Do you not know that to be a lover of the world means enmity with God? Therefore, whoever wants to be a lover of the world makes himself an enemy of God.

JAMES 4:4, NAB

MORNING READING

So let us not "love the world or things in the world" [see 1 Jn 2:15]. Now no one should say, "But the 'things in the world' are things God has made! Why then should I not love what God has made?" All these things are in fact good, but woe to you if you love the things that are made, and forsake their Maker! They are beautiful to see, but how much more beautiful is he who formed them! Do not let Satan sneak up on you, with his typical suggestions, such as: "Enjoy everything that God has made! Why else did he make them except for your enjoyment?" In this way people intoxicate themselves and perish, forgetting their own Creator. For when they use the things he has made lustfully and immoderately, they are despising him.

What a person desires, if he worships it, is to him a god. A vice in the heart is an idol on the altar.

ST. JEROME

FOR REFLECTION

Father, forgive me when I seek your Hand instead of your Face.

EVENING READING

God does not forbid you to love all these things, but he does not want you to trust them to make you happy. Rather, he wants you to approve and praise them so that you may love your Creator. In the same way, my brothers, it is as if a bridegroom made a ring for his bride, and having received the ring, she cherished it more than the bridegroom who made it for her. By all means, let her love what the bridegroom has given her; but should she say, "This ring is enough; I have no desire to see his face now"? What sort of woman would she be? Who would not despise such foolishness?

DAY 14
Only God Abides Forever, and He Must Be Our Dwelling Place

O Lord, you have been our refuge through all generations. Before the mountains were begotten and the earth and the world were brought forth, from everlasting to everlasting you are God. You turn man back to dust, saying, "Return, O children of men."

PSALM 90:1-3, NAB

MORNING READING

Do not be foolish, my soul, and do not let the tumult of your folly deafen the ear of your heart. Listen now: The Word himself calls you to return, and with him is the place of quiet that cannot be disturbed, where your love can never be forsaken unless it first forsakes him. See how the things of this world pass away, so that others may take their place, and the whole universe be made complete in all its parts. "But do I ever pass away?" says the Word of God. Establish your dwelling place in him, my soul; you may safely commit all that you have to him.

Let the world indulge its madness, for it cannot endure and passes like a shadow.... But we, buried deep in the very wounds of Christ, why should we be dismayed?

ST. PETER CANISIUS

FOR REFLECTION

Father, teach me not to waste my love on shadows or to lavish my hope on the wind.

EVENING READING

For even now, my soul, you have become tired of this world's empty deceits. Entrust to the Truth whatever you have of the truth, and you shall lose nothing. What is decayed will once again flourish; what is diseased will be healed; whatever in you is perishable will be transformed and renewed and made whole again. And what is perishable in you will not pull you down to the grave, but will stand with you and abide forever in heaven, before God who abides and endures forever. Why then, my soul, are you being perverse by following the lead of the perishable flesh? Rather let the flesh turn around and follow you.

Each Human Failing Falsely Imitates One of God's Good Qualities

You said in your heart, "I will ascend to heaven.... I will make myself like the Most High." But you are brought down to Sheol, to the depths of the Pit.

ISAIAH 14:13-15

MORNING READING

Vices deceive with a false and shadowy beauty. Pride makes a pretense of superiority, but you alone, Lord, are the highest over all. And what does ambition seek except honor and glory—but you alone are to be honored above all things, and glorious forevermore. The cruelty of the powerful wishes to be feared; but who is to be feared but God only? The enticements of the lustful may claim to be love, yet nothing is more enticing than your love, nor is anything loved more wholesomely than your truth, bright and beautiful above all things. Sloth seems to long for rest, but what sure rest is there besides the Lord? Luxury would fain be called plenty and abundance; but you are the fullness and unfailing plentifulness of unfading joys.

No wickedness, no heresy, not even the devil himself can deceive anyone without counterfeiting virtue.

ST. DOROTHEOS OF GAZA

FOR REFLECTION

Just as the production of counterfeit money only proves the value of true currency, Lord, our counterfeit virtues show how precious are the divine qualities they deceptively imitate.

EVENING READING

Extravagance shows itself off as liberality; but you, Lord, are the most lavish giver of all good. Covetousness desires to possess much, but you possess all things. Envy contends for excellence, but what is so excellent as you? Anger seeks revenge, but who avenges more justly than you? Thus the soul commits fornication when it turns away from you, Lord, seeking those things without you, which it can find pure and untainted nowhere until it returns again to you. Thus all those who separate themselves far from you and raise themselves against you nevertheless perversely imitate you.

DAY 16

When Temptations Arise, God Gives Us Grace to Exercise Self-Control

For the grace of God has appeared, saving all and training us to reject godless ways and worldly desires and to live temperately, justly and devoutly in this age.

TITUS 2:11-12, NAB

MORNING READING

It was my old "mistresses," the most vain and trifling of things, that held me back. They tugged gently at the sleeve of my flesh, and whispered softly in my ear: "Can you really part with us? From this moment on shall we never be with you again?" What impurities, what shameful things they suggested! And then I hardly heard them speaking, for they were not openly contradicting me face to face, but rather stood muttering softly behind my back; and they slyly tugged at me from behind as I left them, trying to make me look back at them. In this way they held me back as I hesitated to shake them loose, snatch myself away, and leap over to the place where you, Lord, were calling me.

A man who governs his passions is master of the world. We must either command them or be enslaved by them. It is better to be a hammer than an anvil.

ST. DOMINIC

FOR REFLECTION

When my old habits whisper to me, Lord, drown out their temptations with the thunder of your voice, calling me to walk with you.

EVENING READING

But by now the voice of my old unruly habit was faint; for in the very direction I had turned, in the place to which I had decided, still trembling, to go, I saw the chaste dignity of Self-Control. She stretched forth those holy hands of hers, full of a multitude of good examples, to receive and embrace me. In her company there were so many young men and maidens, a multitude of youth and of every age with Self-Control herself in their midst, not at all barren, but a fruitful mother of joys—her children by you, Lord, her Husband. And she encouraged me with a playful smile as if to say: "Can't you do what even these young people have done? Why do you stand in your own strength—so that you fail to stand at all? Cast yourself upon him."

Is Obeying God Too Much Work?

Do not toil to acquire wealth; be wise enough to desist. When your eyes light upon it, it is gone; for suddenly it takes to itself wings, flying like an eagle toward heaven.

PROVERBS 23:4-5

MORNING READING

How do we know that we love the children of God? By this: "that we love God and do his commandments" [see 1 Jn 5:2]. Those words may make us groan because we must work so hard to obey God's commandments. But listen to what I have to say: What kind of love truly makes you toil? The love of greed. All the material things you love are the real source of your toil, for there is no toil in loving God. Greed will demand of you labor, danger, hardships and troubles, and you will readily agree to its demands. For what purpose? So that you can have what will fill up your purse but empty out your peace of mind!

He has much who needs least. Do not create necessities for yourself.

VENERABLE JOSE ESCRIVÁ

FOR REFLECTION

Lord, I cannot serve two masters; make me as eager to serve you as I have served Mammon.

EVENING READING

You have found that you were more secure before you accumulated so much. See what greed has imposed on you: You have filled your house, and now you fear burglars. You have hoarded money and lost sleep. See what greed has commanded you: "Do this!" And you did it. But what command has God given you instead? "Love me. You love wealth, but if you seek wealth, you may not find it. Yet I am with those who seek me. You love honors, but you may not attain them. Has anyone ever loved me without attaining me? You want friends in high places, so you go through the people under them to curry their favor. Love me instead: You do not have to seek my help by gaining the favor of anyone else. Your love in itself makes me present to you." What could be sweeter than this love, brothers and sisters?

The Snare of Spiritual Counterfeits

Now the Spirit expressly says that in later times some will depart from the faith by giving heed to deceitful spirits and doctrines of demons, through the pretensions of liars whose consciences are seared.

1 TIMOTHY 4:1-2

MORNING READING

When I was still casting about spiritually, whom could I find to reconcile me to you, Lord? Was I to ask spirits for help? By what prayer? By what rituals? Many who strive to return to you but are not able to do so on their own, I am told, have tried this path, and have fallen into a craving for strange visions; they have been rewarded with delusions. Being arrogant, they sought you with a pride in what they learned, puffing out their chests instead of beating them in penance. And so by a likeness in heart, they drew to themselves the princes of the air, their conspirators and companions in pride, by whom, through the power of magic, they were deceived. For the one they found was the devil, transforming himself into an angel of light.

That the proximate and immediate cause [of modern heresies] consists in an error of the mind cannot be open to doubt. We recognize [however] that the remote causes may be reduced to two: curiosity and pride.

POPE ST. PIUS X

FOR REFLECTION

Lord, how often have I let my craving for novelty, my demand to be entertained, drive me to seek out what will feed my curiosity instead of my soul?

EVENING READING

How wide is the scope of inquisitiveness—the foolish desire to know everything. This is what is at work in spectacles, in theaters, in satanic rites, in the magical arts, in dealings with darkness—none other than idle curiosity. Sometimes it even tempts the servants of God so that they wish to do something miraculous, in order to test God to see whether he will hear their prayers for a miracle. If God has given you the power, go ahead and work a miracle; that is why he gave you the power. But do not think that those who have never worked a miracle are not part of the kingdom of God. For even of certain false prophets the Lord has said: "They shall do signs and wonders" [see Mt 24:24].

"The Season of the Savior's Mercy ..."

Now Is the Time to Repent

DAY 19

We Must Not Delay in
Rousing Ourselves to Repentance

"Today, when you hear his voice, do not harden your hearts" ....
But exhort one another every day, as long as it is called "today,"
that none of you may be hardened by the deceitfulness of sin.

HEBREWS 3:7-8, 13

MORNING READING

Thus with the baggage of the world I was sweetly burdened, like
one who is asleep; and whenever I thought about you, Lord, my
thoughts were like the feeble efforts of those who want to wake
up, but who are still overpowered with a heavy drowsiness, and fall
back into a deep slumber. They are content to sleep on, even
when they know it is time to get up. In the same way, I knew it
was better for me to give myself up to your love than to give
myself over to my own lust. But even though your love satisfied
and persuaded me, my lust pleased me and held me bound.

To sin is human, but to persist in sin is devilish.

ST. CATHERINE OF SIENA

FOR REFLECTION

When the subtle pleasures of my sin lull me to sleep, send me a wake-up call, Lord!

EVENING READING

In this condition of spiritual slumber, I had no answer when you called me, saying: "Awake, you who sleep, and arise from the dead, and Christ will give you light" [see Eph 5:14]. You were showing me on every side that what you said was true; but even though I was convicted by the truth, I had nothing at all to reply but the drowsy and drawling words: "Soon enough; soon enough. Leave me alone a little while longer." But "soon" was not at all soon, and "a little while" went on for a long while. In vain did I "delight in your law in the inner man" while "another law in my members warred against the law of my mind, and brought me into captivity to the law of sin that is in my members" [see Rom 7:22, 23]. For the law of sin is the force of habit, by which the mind is drawn along and held, even against its will—and rightly so, because it has willingly fallen into the habit.

DAY 20

No One Knows When Judgment Will Come ... Embrace Christ's Mercy Now

Therefore you also must be ready; for the Son of man is coming at an hour you do not expect.

MATTHEW 24:44

MORNING READING

Christ is come, but first to save, and then to judge: to sentence to punishment those who refused to be saved; to bring to life those who, by believing, did not reject salvation. In this way, then, our Lord came first as Medicine, not as Judge. For if he had come to judge first, he would have found no one on whom he might bestow the rewards of righteousness. Since, then, he saw that all were sinners, and that no one was exempt from the sentence of death that followed sin, his mercy had to be sought first, before his judgment could be executed.

We must busy ourselves with preparations for our departure from this world. For even if the day when the whole world ends never overtakes us, the end of each of us is right at the door.

ST. JOHN CHRYSOSTOM

FOR REFLECTION

My life on earth could come to an end this evening, Lord; would I be ready to meet you as my Judge?

EVENING READING

Let everyone, then, wisely receive the admonitions of the Master, before the season of the Savior's mercy passes by—a season that is now in blossom, as long as the human race is spared. For the reason we are spared is that we may be converted rather than condemned. Only God knows when the end of the world will come; nevertheless, now is the time for faith. Whether any of us here will be around at the end of the world, I do not know; perhaps the end will not find us. Even so, our own end is very near to each of us, since we are mortal. No doubt through our frailness we walk daily in fear of the accidents inherent in life; and even if these accidents do not occur, time goes on. However long we may be spared, in the end, old age comes, and there is no way of putting that off. For that reason, we must listen to the Lord.

DAY 21
God Sometimes Uses Adversity
to Lead Us Back to Him

*Day and night your hand was heavy upon me; my strength was
dried up as by the heat of summer. Then I acknowledged my sin to
you, my guilt I covered not. I said, "I confess my faults to the
Lord," and you took away the guilt of my sin.*

PSALM 32:4-5, NAB

MORNING READING

I was a poor fool, seething like the sea. Forsaking you, Lord, I
followed the violent course of my own torrents. I rushed past all
your lawful bounds, and I did not escape your scourges. For what
mortal can escape them? But you were always beside me,
mercifully angry, ruining all my illicit pleasures with bitter
discontent—all to draw me on so that I might instead seek
pleasures that were free from discontent. But where could I find
such pleasures except in you, Lord? I could find them only in you,
who teaches us by sorrow, and wounds us in order to heal us, and
kills us so that we may not die apart from you.

God measures out affliction according to our need.

ST. JOHN CHRYSOSTOM

FOR REFLECTION

Is there some adversity in my life, Jesus—however small—that I can use as an occasion to draw closer to you?

EVENING READING

You humble the proud, who are like those wounded. Through my own bloated pride I was separated from you; yes, my face was so swollen that my eyes were shut and blinded. Yet even though you, Lord, are the same forever and ever, you do not remain angry with us forever. For you take pity on us, who are only dust and ashes. It was pleasing in your sight to transform what was deformed in me; and by inward stings you disturbed me, so that I would be dissatisfied until I could see you clearly with the eye of my soul. By the secret hand of your healing my swelling was relieved; and the disordered and darkened eye of my mind was day by day made whole by the stinging salve of a healthy sorrow.

DAY 22
We Cannot Hide From God

If I say, "Surely the darkness shall hide me, and night shall be my light"—For you darkness itself is not dark, and night shines as the day.

PSALM 139:11-12, NAB

MORNING READING

The unrighteous may depart and flee from you without rest as fast as they can; yet you will still see them and pierce through the shadows. And how do they think to have harmed you by fleeing? How do they think to have discredited your rule, which from the highest heavens to the lowest depths of the earth is most just and perfect? Where did they flee when they fled from your presence? Where would you be unable to find them? But they ran away so that they might not see you seeing them—so that, blinded, they might stumble into you. You stay close to all that you have made, so that the unjust might stumble into you, and be justly hurt, retreating from your gentleness and backing into your justice, and falling into the consequences of their own rough ways.

Lord, my God, you are not a stranger to the one who does not estrange himself from you. How do they say that it is you who absent yourself?

ST. JOHN OF THE CROSS

FOR REFLECTION

The world can never be my hiding place from you, Lord; so let me make you my hiding place from the world.

EVENING READING

You hide your heart from other people; hide it from God if you can! How can you hide from the One to whom a sinner once prayed—confessing in fear—"Where shall I go from your Spirit? And where shall I flee from your face?" He sought a way to flee, to escape the judgment of God, but he found none. For what place could he go where God was not already there? So where will you go? Where will you flee? Would you like some advice? If you want to flee from him, flee to him instead. Flee to him by confessing to him; do not flee from him by trying to hide. For you cannot hide, but you can confess. Tell him, "You are the place to which I flee for refuge," and let love be nourished in you, because love alone leads to life.

When We Sin, We Imitate the Devil

Jesus said to them, "If God were your Father, you would love me....
You are of your father the devil, and your will is to do your
father's desires."

JOHN 8:42, 44

MORNING READING

"Whoever commits sin is of the devil, for the devil sins from the
beginning" [see 1 Jn 3:8]. What does St. John mean when he says
"of the devil"? He means that the sinner is imitating the devil. For
the devil has never made anyone or begotten anyone or created
anyone; but whoever acts as the devil does becomes in one sense a
child of the devil, as if begotten by him. The child resembles the
father, not because they are literally kin, but because the child
imitates the father. And you, too, if you imitate the devil through
pride and irreverence toward God, will be a child of the devil.

When the devil is called the god of this world, it is not because he
made it, but because we serve him with our worldliness.

ST. THOMAS AQUINAS

FOR REFLECTION

Father, I renounce my kinship to the devil through sin, and claim my adoption by you through the work of Christ.

EVENING READING

All sinners are born of the devil inasmuch as they are sinners. Adam was made by God, but when he consented to the devil, he was born of the devil, and his descendants are all like him. Out of that first condemnation we are born. For if we were born without sin, why would we run with our babies to be baptized for the forgiveness of sin? Brothers, mark well, then, the two kinds of parentage from which we are born: that of Adam, and that of Christ. Both are men, but one of them is only a man, and the other is also God. Through the man who is God we have been made righteous. Our birth in Adam cast us down into death; our birth in Christ has raised us up to life. One birth has brought with it sin; the other has set us free from sin.

DAY 24
We Must Imitate God's Mercy

*Be angry but do not sin; do not let the sun go down on your anger,
and give no opportunity to the devil.*

EPHESIANS 4:26

MORNING READING

Now do not think that anger is insignificant. And what is anger?
The desire for vengeance. Imagine: We desire to be avenged,
when even Christ himself has not yet been avenged, nor have the
martyrs been avenged. The patience of God still waits, so that the
enemies of Christ, the enemies of the martyrs, might be converted. So who are we, that we should seek vengeance? If God
should seek vengeance against us for our own offenses, where
could we hide? Even the One who has never done us harm in any
way does not seek vengeance against us—yet are we seeking to be
avenged, we who almost daily are offending God? So forgive;
forgive from the heart.

*If an angry man raises the dead, God is still displeased with
his anger.*

ABBA AGATHO

FOR REFLECTION

Who is it, Father, that I need to forgive even now before my anger festers into hatred?

EVENING READING

Do not sin by keeping anger in your heart—for if you do keep it, you are storing up anger against yourself. What is hatred, after all, but anger that is allowed to remain, that has become ingrained and deep-rooted. What was anger when it was fresh becomes hatred when it is aged. Anger is a "splinter," hatred, a "log." We sometimes find fault with someone who is angry while we retain hatred in our own hearts; and so Christ said to us: "You see the splinter in your brother's eye, and do you fail to see the log in your own eye?" [see Mt 7:3-5]. How did the splinter grow into a log? Because it was not at once pulled out. Because you left it lying there. Through evil suspicions you watered it, and by watering you nourished it, and by nourishing it you grew it into a beam.

"Prepare a Place for Love ..."

Learn First to Fear God

DAY 25
We Must Fear God Before
We Can Love Him

*Behold, the eye of the Lord is on those who fear him, on those who
hope in his steadfast love.*

PSALM 33:18

MORNING READING

The fear of God prepares a place for love. But once love has begun
to dwell in our hearts, the fear that prepared the place for it is
driven out. As the one increases, the other decreases; and the
more love fills us, the less place there is for fear. Greater love, less
fear; greater fear, less love. But if there is no fear at all, there is no
way for love to come in. As we can see in sewing, the needle
introduces the thread into the cloth. The needle goes in, but the
thread cannot follow unless the needle comes out first. In the
same way, the fear of God first occupies our minds, but it does not
remain there, because it enters only in order to introduce love.

*Christ joined the law of fear with that of love. The incompleteness
of the fear of punishment was taken away by love, and what
remained was the perfection of holy fear, that is, fear simply of
sinning, not because of personal damnation, but because sin is an
insult to [God], the supreme Goodness.*

ST. CATHERINE OF SIENA

FOR REFLECTION

Lord God, prune my heart with a holy fear that will make room for love to blossom and bear fruit.

EVENING READING

The fear of God wounds us like a surgeon's knife. It cuts out the festering flesh and seems to make the wound even larger. Yet while the wound festered, even though it was smaller, it was more dangerous. In a similar way, once the knife cuts, the wound hurts more than it did before. Having the operation is more painful than not having it. But such healing surgery inflicts pain only so that the wound may never hurt again once it is healed. For that reason, let the fear of God occupy your heart, so that it may bring charity; let the wound heal into a scar. God is such a Physician that he does not even leave any scars—only put yourself under his care. Fear is the surgery, love is the good health that follows.

DAY 26
There Are Two Kinds of Fear of God, But One Lasts Forever

There is no fear in love, but perfect love drives out fear.

1 JOHN 4:18

The fear of the Lord is pure, enduring forever.

PSALM 19:10, NAB

MORNING READING

There are those who fear God because they fear to be cast into hell to burn with the devil in everlasting fire. This is the fear that introduces love; it comes so that it may leave again once love is there. For if you still fear God only because of his punishments, you do not yet love him. You are not longing for what is good, but only fleeing what is bad. Nevertheless, because you are afraid of what is bad, you change your ways and begin to desire what is good. And once that happens, the fear within you is pure. But what is this pure fear? The fear of losing what is good. Only when you fear that you may lose God's presence are you embracing him and longing to enjoy God himself.

Perfect love ... leads a man on to perfect fear. Such a man fears and keeps to God's will, not for fear of punishment, not to avoid condemnation, but ... because he has tasted the sweetness of being with God; he fears he may fall away from it.

ST. DOROTHEOS OF GAZA

FOR REFLECTION

What kind of fear do I have, Lord? Do I fear to face you or to lose you?

EVENING READING

Suppose there are two married women. One of them wants to commit adultery and enjoys the prospect of it, but she fears that her husband will condemn her. She fears her husband, but only because she loves wickedness. She is not grateful for her husband's presence, but burdened by it, and if she lives sinfully, she fears his coming. On the other hand, consider a wife who loves her husband, who feels that she owes him pure embraces and refuses to be stained by adultery. She longs for her husband's presence. Now both women fear their husbands, but the one fears his coming, and the other fears his going. One fears being condemned, the other fears being forsaken. The first is the fear that love must cast out, and the second is the pure fear that endures forever.

DAY 27
We Praise God Through
Our Humble Confessions

If we confess our sins, he is faithful and just, and will forgive our sins and cleanse us from all unrighteousness.

1 JOHN 1:9

MORNING READING

Let the arrogant laugh at me, and those whom you have not yet cast down and broken in heart for the sake of their salvation, my God. Nevertheless, I will confess to you my shame in order to give you praise. Bear with me, I beg you, and give me grace to retrace in my memory now the wandering errors of my past, and to offer you the sacrifice of joy. For what am I without you, but a guide to my own downfall? Or what am I, even at my best, but an infant suckling your milk, and feeding on you, the Food that never perishes? But what indeed is any human being, being only human? The strong and the mighty may laugh at us if they wish, but let us who are weak and needy confess to you.

There has never yet been a bomb invented that is half so powerful as one mortal sin.

THOMAS MERTON

FOR REFLECTION

Lord, if only we could see the corrosive effects of our sins rippling out from our hearts, our words, our hands—how might we be ashamed and run to you in repentance!

EVENING READING

Accept the sacrifice of my confessions from my tongue, which you have formed and stirred up to praise your name. Heal all my bones and let them say, "O Lord, who is like you?" [see Ps 35:10]. It is not as if the one who confesses to you teaches you about what is going on inside him. For a closed heart does not shut out your eye, nor can our hardheartedness thrust away your hands, for you soften it as you will, either in mercy or in justice to us, and "there is nothing that can hide itself from your heat" [see Ps 19:6]. But let my soul praise you, that it may love you; and let it confess your own mercies to you, that it may praise you.

DAY 28

We Bring Healing and Encouragement to Others When We Confess Our Struggles and Victories

Confess your sins to one another, and pray for one another, that you may be healed.

JAMES 5:16

MORNING READING

"You desire truth," and "whoever does the truth comes to the light" [see Ps 51:6; Jn 3:21]. This is what I wish to do through confession in my heart before you in prayer, and before many witnesses through my writings. Lord, the depths of the human conscience are laid bare before your eyes; what in me, then, could possibly be hidden from you, even if I were unwilling to confess it to you? In failing to confess, I would only hide you from myself, not myself from you. To you, then, Lord, I am laid bare, whatever I am—and what a profit there is in confessing to you.

The demon which by your silence you let dwell in your heart has been killed because you confessed your sin.... Henceforth he shall never make a home in you, because you have thrown him out of doors into the open air.

ABBA THEONAS

FOR REFLECTION

Help me, Father, to fling open the doors of my heart in confession, letting in the fresh air, and the sunlight, and you.

EVENING READING

My most secret Physician, you make clear to me what benefits can be gained by confessing my struggles to others. No doubt you have forgiven and covered my past sins, so that you might make me blessed in you, transforming my soul by faith and your sacrament. But when I confess these in a way that they may be read and heard, they may stir up the hearts of others. My confession may encourage others not to sleep in despair, saying, "I cannot"; it may provoke them instead to wake up in the love of your mercy and the sweetness of your grace—by which the one who is weak is made strong, provided he is made conscious of his own weakness. As for those who are good, they will take delight in hearing about the past errors of someone who is now freed from them.

We Must Remember That We Are Dependent on God's Grace

The complacence of fools destroys them; but he who listens to me will dwell secure and will be at ease, without dread of evil.

PROVERBS 1:32-33

MORNING READING

Deep within us we may find the evil of self-complacency. This is the vanity of all those who are pleased with themselves even when they fail to please others, or have no desire to please others, or even work hard to displease others. But in being so pleased with themselves they displease you deeply, Lord—not merely by priding themselves on qualities that are not good, as if they were good; but also by taking pleasure in your good gifts as if these gifts were of their own creation; or else by admitting that these gifts are from you, yet still claiming that they have earned them through their own merits. Or even if they should know that they have received these gifts by your grace alone, they envy your grace to others and will not rejoice with them in it.

A holy man used to weep bitterly whenever he saw someone sinning; he would say: "He today; I tomorrow."

THE SAYINGS OF THE FATHERS

FOR REFLECTION

No other person can see inside my heart, Lord, and even I fail to see into every dark chamber there. Only you know every corner of who I am; please reveal me to myself.

EVENING READING

This is how I appear to myself, but I may well be deceived. For there is a lamentable darkness in which my true capabilities are so concealed that when my mind speculates about its own powers, it hesitates to trust its own judgment—because what is truly inside is largely obscure unless experience brings it to light. Thus no one should feel secure in this life, because the whole of it is one long test; and no one who has been able to pass from a worse state to a better can be certain that he will not later also pass from a better state to a worse. Our only hope, our only confidence, our only assured promise, Lord, is your mercy.

The Struggles and Trials of Life Should Drive Us to the Mercy of God

Withhold not, O Lord, your compassion from me; may your kindness and your truth ever preserve me. For all about me are evils beyond reckoning; my sins so overcome me that I cannot see; they are more numerous than the hairs of my head, and my heart fails me.

PSALM 41:12-13, NAB

MORNING READING

When at last I shall be united to you with all that I am, then I shall feel no more pain or labor. Then my life shall be truly alive, being full of you in every way. You raise up all those whose lives you fill, but because I am not yet full of you, I am a burden to myself. For now, the things I wrongly enjoy, over which I should grieve, are in a struggle with the things I rightly grieve, which should give me cause for joy—and on which side the victory may lie I do not know. Woe is me! Lord, have pity on me. Behold, I do not hide my wounds. You are the doctor, I am the patient; you are merciful, and I am miserable.

Thank the good God for having visited you through suffering. If we knew the value of suffering, we would ask for it.

BLESSED BROTHER ANDRE

FOR REFLECTION

If I had never known adversity, Lord, I might never have known the depths of your mercy.

EVENING READING

Isn't our life on earth an ordeal? Does anyone ever wish for troubles and difficulties? You command, Lord, that we endure these things, but not that we love them; for no one loves what he has to endure. Yet even if he takes joy in his ability to endure, he prefers that there would be nothing to endure in the first place. In adversity, I desire prosperity; in prosperity, I fear adversity. What middle place is there, then, between these, where life is not a trial? There is grief in the prosperity of this world, in the fear of misfortune, in the fading of joy. There is grief in the adversity of this world, as we desire prosperity—because adversity itself is a hard thing to bear, and it makes a shipwreck of endurance! Isn't life a trial, and that without ceasing? My entire hope, Lord, is only in your exceedingly great mercy!

"For Now, We Are Still Fighting ..."

The Struggle for Holiness

Sinful Habits Cause Our New Nature in Christ to Struggle Against Our Old Nature

I can will what is right, but I cannot do it. For I do not do the good I want, but the evil I do not want is what I do.

ROMANS 7:18-19

MORNING READING

I was bound, not with the irons of another, but with the iron bonds of my own will. The enemy was master of my will, and had made of it a chain, and had bound me tightly. For out of my perverse will grew lust; and lust indulged became habit; and habit unresisted became necessity. By these links, as it were, forged together (that is why I call it a chain), a hard slavery held me captive. But that new will that had begun to develop in me—a will to worship you freely and to enjoy you, my God, the only sure joy—was not yet able to overcome my former willfulness, made strong by long indulgence. Thus did my two wills, one old and the other new, one fleshly and the other spiritual, struggle within me; and by their battle they tore my soul in two.

Our self-will is so subtle and so deeply rooted within us, so covered with excuses and defended by false reasoning, that it seems to be a demon. When we cannot do our own will in one way, we do it in another, under all kinds of pretexts.

ST. CATHERINE OF GENOA

FOR REFLECTION

Train my will, Father, to obey you in the little things, so that I can cultivate a habit of holiness.

EVENING READING

Thus I came to understand, from my own experience, what I had read, how "the flesh lusts against the spirit, and the spirit against the flesh" [see Gal 5:17]. I truly fought both ways, yet more on the side of the desires which I approved in myself rather than those which I disapproved in myself. For in the latter it was no longer really I who was involved, because here I suffered against my will rather than willingly. And yet it was through my own actions that habit had become a stronger adversary against me, because I had willingly come to be what I now found myself unwilling to be. Who, then, with any justice can object when such just punishment follows the sinner?

We Have Only Begun to Become Righteous

I have fought the good fight, I have finished the race, I have kept the faith. Henceforth there is laid up for me the crown of righteousness, which the Lord, the righteous judge, will award to me on that Day, and not only to me but also to all who have loved his appearing.

2 TIMOTHY 4:7-8

MORNING READING

There is no perfect righteousness except among the angels, and hardly in the angels, if you compare them to God. In us, righteousness has only just begun, by faith and through the Spirit. And the beginning of our righteousness is the confession of sins. Have you begun to stop trying to defend your sins? Then you have made a beginning of righteousness. But it will be perfected in you when the day comes that this is all you desire, when "death will be swallowed up in victory" [see 1 Cor 15:54], when you will no longer itch with wrong desires, when you will no longer struggle with flesh and blood, when you will receive the trophy of victory, the triumph over the enemy. Then you will have perfect righteousness.

What, then, does God watch with pleasure and delight? The man who is fighting for him against riches, against the world, against hell, against himself.

ST. LOUIS MARIE DE MONTFORT

FOR REFLECTION

How can I lose the fight, Lord, as long as you are inside the ring fighting with me and outside the ring cheering me on?

EVENING READING

For now, we are still fighting. While we fight, we remain in the ring; we box and are boxed. Whether we shall win remains to be seen, but the one who wins is the one who, even when he belts his opponent, does not rely on his own strength, but on God—who is cheering him on. The devil is all alone when he fights against us, and if we try to fight alone, the devil will beat us. But if we fight with God on our side, we will overcome. The devil is a skillful enemy; how many trophies he has already won! What are we to do, then, considering how well practiced he is? Call on the Almighty to help you against the devil's strategies. Let the One who cannot be overcome live in you, and you will surely overcome the one who has so often beaten others.

DAY 33

Do Not Give Up the Struggle for Holiness; God's Reward, Eternal Life, Is Waiting for Us

He who sows to the Spirit will from the Spirit reap eternal life. And let us not grow weary in well-doing, for in due season we shall reap, if we do not lose heart.

GALATIANS 6:8-9

MORNING READING

Listen now, and do not give up! If you are growing weary in your labors, let the promised wages make you strong. Who would work hard in a vineyard while forgetting the wages he has been promised? If he forgets that, his hands stop their work. But calling to mind the promised reward presses him to persevere in his labors. Now even in that situation, the one who promises to pay the wages is only a man who can lie about them. How much more determined should you be, then, to work hard in God's field, when the One who has promised you a reward is the Truth himself! Unlike a human employer, God cannot die or be replaced or cheat you out of your wages.

Nothing seems tiresome or painful when you are working for a Master who pays well; who rewards even a cup of cold water given for love of him.

ST. DOMINIC SAVIO

FOR REFLECTION

You are not only the Master for whom I labor, Lord; you are also my shade tree and my cup of cold water in the heat of the day.

EVENING READING

And what is God's promise? Is it gold, which people in this life love so much, or silver? Is it possessions, for which people extravagantly spend their gold, however much they may love it? Is it pleasant estates, spacious homes, a host of servants, countless livestock? No—it is not for such wages as these that he exhorts us to endure in our labors. Instead, this is what God promises: eternal life! So let no one seduce you into choosing death instead. Long for the promise of eternal life. What can the world promise? Let it promise you what it will; it is making that promise to someone who may die tomorrow. And when you die, how will you face the One who lives forever?

God's Grace Empowers Us to Control Our Physical Appetites

"All things are lawful for me," but I will not be enslaved by anything. "Food is meant for the stomach and the stomach for food"—and God will destroy both one and the other. The body is not meant for immorality, but for the Lord, and the Lord for the body.

1 CORINTHIANS 6:12-13

MORNING READING

There is yet another "evil of the day" that I wish were "sufficient" to it [see Mt 6:34]. For by eating and drinking we restore the daily losses of the body, until the day comes when you destroy both food and stomach; when you will slay this emptiness of mine with a marvelous fullness; when you will clothe this corruptible nature with eternal and incorruptible life. But for now this necessity is sweet to me, and against this sweetness must I fight, so that I might not be made captive by it. I carry on my daily war by fastings, "bringing my body into subjection." This much you have taught me: that I must look upon food as medicine.

Irrational feeding darkens the soul and makes it unfit for spiritual experiences.

ST. THOMAS AQUINAS

FOR REFLECTION

Lord, I have no choice but to live with my appetite; teach me how to live with it as my servant, and not as my master.

EVENING READING

Placed, then, in the midst of these temptations, I strive daily against craving for food and drink. For it is not the kind of temptation I am able to deal with simply by resolving to cut it off once and for all, never to touch it again, as I was able to do with fornication. The throat is a bridle, then, that must be held with a hand neither too firm nor too slack. And who, Lord, is not to some degree carried away beyond the bounds of necessity in what he eats and drinks? Whoever he is, he is great; let him magnify your name. But I am not such a one, for I am a sinful man. Yet I also magnify your name, and he who has overcome the world makes intercession to you for my sins, counting me among the weak members of his body.

Our Love for Praise Can Lead Us to Sin

Do nothing out of selfishness or out of vainglory; rather, humbly regard others as more important than yourselves.

PHILIPPIANS 2:3, NAB

MORNING READING

I am delighted with praise, but more with the truth itself than with praise. For if I had to choose between, on the one hand, being utterly mistaken or even insane, yet praised by all, and on the other hand, being fully assured of the truth, yet blamed by all, I know that I would choose the latter. Nevertheless, there is a dangerous temptation to the love of praise in what others say about us and what they know about our actions. It leads us to try to establish a high reputation for ourselves, and then to go around collecting the compliments we have solicited.

If you glory in yourself and not in the Lord, you will be kissing your own hand instead of the hand of your Benefactor.

ST. BERNARD OF CLAIRVAUX

FOR REFLECTION

Lord, let me walk through the day gathering gratefully any compliments I may receive, so that I can make of them every evening a bouquet of praise to be cast at your feet.

EVENING READING

"Beware of practicing your righteousness before men in order to be seen by them" [see Mt 6:1]. Does the Lord say here that you must hide the good you do from others and fear to be seen by them? But if you have no onlookers, you will have no imitators, either. So your good works should be seen. But you must not do them simply for the sake of being seen. That should not be the source of your pleasure, the reason for rejoicing, so that you think you have enjoyed the full fruit of your good deed when you have been seen and praised. That is nothing at all. Call yourself unworthy when you are praised; let the praise be given to the One who is in you and working through you. Do not, then, do your good works for the sake of your own praise, but rather to the praise of him who has given you the power to do good.

True Happiness Lies in Knowing the Truth, Even When It Exposes Sin

The light has come into the world, and men loved darkness rather than light, because their deeds were evil. For every one who does evil hates the light, and does not come to the light, lest his deeds should be exposed.

JOHN 3:19-20

MORNING READING

For a happy life comes from joy in the truth. Everyone wants this happy life; joy in the truth is what all people want. So why, then, does truth sometimes engender hatred? Why does the servant of God come to be an enemy of those who also want a happy life, even though true happiness is joy in the truth? It must be that our love of truth is such that when we love something that is not the truth, we pretend to ourselves that what we love is the truth. Then, because we hate to be proved wrong, we are unwilling to be convinced that we have deceived ourselves.

Those who wage war against the truth are powerless to win; rather, they wound themselves, like those who kick against spikes.

ST. JOHN CHRYSOSTOM

FOR REFLECTION
Father, what truth am I trying to hide from today?

EVENING READING

In this way, then, people hate the truth for the sake of whatever it is they love instead of the truth. They love truth when it shines warmly on them, and hate it when it rebukes them. Because they are unwilling to be deceived, and yet wish to deceive others, they love truth when it is revealed to them and hate it when it uncovers them. On this account, truth will repay them what they deserve: Those who are not willing to be exposed by it will nevertheless be exposed against their will, while the truth itself will be concealed from them. Truly, this is how the human mind is: Blind and sick, shameful and ill-behaved, it desires to lie hidden, but does not wish for anything to be hidden from it. And yet the very opposite is what happens: The mind itself lies exposed to the truth, while the truth is hidden from the mind.

"He Is the One I Seek ..."

*God's Word and Sacraments
Deepen Our Faith*

If We Long for Truth, the Father Will Show Us Christ, His Wisdom

Jesus said to him, "I am the way, and the truth, and the life; no one comes to the Father, but by me."

JOHN 14:6

MORNING READING

Let Truth Himself, the Light of my heart, speak to me, and not my own darkness! I had fallen into that darkness and had been blinded by it. But even there, in its depths, I came to love you, Lord. Even when I went astray, I remembered you. I heard your voice behind me, calling me to return, though I could hardly hear it above the din of my own passions. And now, see how I am returning, burning and panting for your fountain. Let no one keep me away; there I will drink and live. Do not let me try to live my own life, for when I lived on my own without you, I lived badly. I was death to myself, but now I have been revived in you. Speak to me; talk with me. I have believed your Scriptures, but their words are sometimes too deep for me.

When you seek truth you seek God whether you know it or not.

BLESSED THERESIA BENEDICTA

FOR REFLECTION

When I search the sacred pages, Lord, show me yourself waiting there among them, ready to correct and comfort, to counsel and command.

EVENING READING

Father, let the secrets of your Word be opened to me when I knock. I beg this of you through our Lord Jesus Christ, your Son, the One through whom you sought us, even when we were not seeking you—who sought us so that we might seek you; your Word, through whom you have made all things, including me; your only-begotten Son, through whom you have called a believing people to adoption, and me among them. I beg you through him, who sits at your right hand, and makes intercession for us, "in whom are hidden all treasures of wisdom and knowledge" [see Col 2:3]. He is the One I seek in your books.

Faith Requires Belief in That Which Cannot Be Proven or Fully Understand

Now faith is the assurance of things hoped for, the conviction of things not seen.

HEBREWS 11:1

MORNING READING

The Catholic Church commanded that certain things should be believed that were not proven. Lord, little by little, with a most gentle, most merciful hand, drawing and calming my heart, you persuaded me to believe. For I considered all the multitude of things that I believed in, even though I had not witnessed them myself: the events of history; accounts of places and cities I had not seen; and all the things I believed simply on the word of friends, or doctors, or other acquaintances. Unless we took all these things on faith, we could accomplish nothing in this life. When I took all this into consideration, you persuaded me, Lord, that I should find fault, not with those who believe your Scriptures, which you have established with such great authority among nearly all nations, but rather with those who do not believe in them.

Faith seeks understanding. I do not seek to understand so that I may believe, but I believe in order to understand.

ST. ANSELM

FOR REFLECTION
Lord, I believe; help my unbelief!

EVENING READING
Spiritual persons, then, judge spiritually. But it is not right for them to act as a judge over your Scripture, Lord, even when there is something in it that they do not understand. Instead, we must submit our understanding to your Scripture, believing with certainty that even what is hidden from our sight is still rightly and truly spoken. For in this way, even those who are now spiritual—who have been renewed in the knowledge of God according to the image of the One who created them—should nevertheless be doers of the law rather than its judges.

Scripture Calls Both the Wise and Simple to Conversion

From childhood you have been acquainted with the sacred writings which are able to instruct you for salvation through faith in Christ Jesus. All scripture is inspired by God and profitable for teaching, for reproof, for correction, and for training in righteousness.

2 TIMOTHY 3:15-16

MORNING READING

Although the Bible can easily be read by all, it hides away the majesty of its secrets within its profound meanings. It stoops to all through a great plainness of language and simplicity of style, yet it demands the close attention of the most serious-minded. In this way it receives all into its wide embrace. It stands upon the height of authority, yet it has allured multitudes into its bosom by a lowliness that is holy. How wonderful is the depth of your Scriptures, Lord. Their surface lies before us, inviting the little ones; and yet, what a marvelous deepness, my God, a marvelous deepness! How awesome to look into it—an awe of honor, and a trembling of love!

But for the searching and right understanding of the Scriptures there is need of a good life and a pure soul, and for Christian virtue to guide the mind to grasp, so far as human nature can, the truth concerning God the Word.

ST. ATHANASIUS

FOR REFLECTION

Lord, let your Scriptures be a mirror, in which I see my infirmities clearly, and a doorway, through which I walk into your presence to be healed.

EVENING READING

Lord, I have known no other book so destructive of pride, so powerful against your enemies and against those who defend themselves, refusing to be reconciled to you, by trying to justify their sins. Lord, I know of no other words so pure, so capable of persuading me to confess my sins to you, and to make my neck submissive to your yoke, and to invite me to serve you with no reward other than yourself. Let me understand these words, good Father. Grant this to me, for I am submitted to your words, and you have established them for the sake of those who are submitted to them.

DAY 40
We Must Ask God to Open the Scriptures to Our Understanding

Open my eyes, that I may consider the wonders of your law. I am a wayfarer of earth; hide not your commands from me. My soul is consumed with longing for your ordinances at all times.

PSALM 119:18-20, NAB

MORNING READING

Let your Scriptures be my chaste delight. Don't let me be deceived by them or deceive others using them. Lord, hear me and have mercy on me—Lord my God, Light of the blind, Strength of the weak, the Light of those who see, the Strength of those who are strong! Listen to my soul, and hear me crying to you out of the deep. For if your ears cannot hear us in the depths, where can we go? To whom can we cry? "The day is yours, and the night also is yours" [see Ps 74:16]. The moments fly by at your bidding. Grant me, then, between those moments a chance to meditate on the hidden things of your law, and do not close the door of your law to those of us who knock.

The one who is well-grounded in the testimonies of the Scripture is the bulwark of the Church.

ST. JEROME

FOR REFLECTION

Father, help me find in the swirling sea of my daily labors an island of grace, however small, where I can meditate on your Word.

EVENING READING

For you have not willed that the deep mysteries of so many pages should have been written in vain. Your Scripture is like a deep forest, and there are those who, like deer, have withdrawn there to be refreshed, where they roam, and walk, and feed, and lie down to chew on what they have found. Perfect me, Lord, and reveal their secrets to me. See how your voice is my joy; your voice surpasses all the abundance of my pleasures. Give me the wisdom that I love, for I do love it, and this love of wisdom is itself a gift from you. Do not abandon your gifts, or despise the grass that thirsts for you. Let me confess to you everything I find in your Book, and let me hear the voice of your praise. Let me drink you in and consider the wonderful things in your law.

The Holy Spirit Must Be Our Inner Teacher

"If you love me, you will keep my commandments. And I will pray the Father, and he will give you another Counselor, to be with you for ever, even the Spirit of truth…. When the Spirit of truth comes, he will guide you into all the truth."

JOHN 14:15-17; 16:13

MORNING READING

"And you have no need that anyone teach you, because his anointing teaches you about everything" [see 1 Jn 2:27]. Though the sound of my words strikes your ear, the Teacher is within you. Do not suppose that anyone really learns something from another human being. I can admonish you by the sound of my voice, but if there is not One within you who teaches, then my words are only meaningless noise. Haven't you all heard this homily before? Yet how many of you will leave this place untaught! Those to whom the Anointing has not spoken within—those whom the Holy Spirit has not taught within—will go back home having learned nothing.

Teaching unsupported by grace may enter our ears, but it never reaches the heart. When God's grace does touch our innermost minds to bring understanding, then his Word, which is received by the ear, can sink deep into the heart.

ST. ISIDORE OF SEVILLE

FOR REFLECTION

Holy Spirit, my inner Teacher, open me to the wisdom of those around me so that I never cease learning your lessons.

EVENING READING

The instruction that comes from others is a kind of help, a call for attention. But the One who truly teaches the heart teaches from heaven. That is why Jesus himself says in the Gospel: "Call no one on earth your teacher; one alone is your Teacher—the Christ" [see Mt 23:10]. So let the Lord himself speak to you within, where no human being can be. The words of instruction I speak from outside, brothers, are what a gardener is to a tree. He works from the outside; he waters it and labors to care for it. Yet no matter how he cultivates the tree, is he the one who forms the apples? Does he clothe the naked limbs with their shady covering of leaves? Does he do any of these things that must come from within? "I have planted, Apollos has watered, but God gave the increase" [see 1 Cor 3:6].

God Nourishes Us Through the Sacraments

For as many of you as were baptized into Christ have put on Christ.

GALATIANS 3:27

MORNING READING

You cannot grow in physical stature simply by willing it, any more than you can choose to be born. But if you had the power to choose to be born, then you could also choose to grow—and that is how it is with your spiritual life. No one can be "born of water and the Spirit" [see Jn 3:5] without willing it; therefore, spiritual growth or decline is also a matter of the will. If you know that you have had a spiritual birth, then recognize that you are an infant, and in order to grow, you must eagerly cling to the breasts of your mother. Now your mother is the Church, and her breasts are the two Testaments of the divine Scriptures. Suckle them to drink the milk of all the sacraments.

The sacramental life cannot be reduced to a set of words and ritual gestures. The sacraments are expressions of faith, hope and love.... Sacramental worship has its natural continuation in the flourishing of Christian life.

POPE JOHN PAUL II

FOR REFLECTION

Even if I receive the sacred mysteries of your Church, Jesus, if I have no love, I am nothing.

EVENING READING

Those who are baptized have received the sacrament of new birth through which they are born of God. Consider what a sacrament it is: It is great, divine, holy, beyond description—and it can make us into new people by the forgiveness of our sins! Nevertheless, those who are baptized must look deeply into their own hearts to see whether the "birth" accomplished in their bodies has also been accomplished in their hearts. They must see whether they have love, and if they do, then they can say, "I am born of God." If they do not have love, then they may be wearing the soldier's uniform, but they are actually wandering deserters from the army. They must have love, or else they must not claim to be born of God.

"Love, and Do What You Want ..."

*Love Is the Root and Fruit of
Our Life With God*

DAY 43
Our Actions Will Be Judged by
Our Loving Intentions

The Lord ... will bring to light what is hidden in darkness and will manifest the motives of our hearts.

1 CORINTHIANS 4:5, NAB

MORNING READING

"He who did not spare his own Son but delivered him up for us all" [see Rom 8:32]. The Father gave Christ into the hands of his enemies; Judas gave him to them as well; does it not seem as if they did the same thing? Judas was a traitor; is God the Father also a traitor? God forbid! you say. St. Paul also writes: "the Son of God loved me and delivered himself up for me" [see Gal 2:20]. If the Father gave up the Son, and the Son gave up himself, what has Judas done? What is it that distinguishes these actions? This is the difference: What the Father and the Son did in love, Judas did in treacherous betrayal. So you see that it is not simply what we do that must be considered, but the thoughts and intentions with which we do it.

At the end of our life, we shall be judged by love.

ST. JOHN OF THE CROSS

FOR REFLECTION

How much of what I do, Father, is rooted in love, and how much is rooted in a selfishness that mimics love in order to get its own way?

EVENING READING

Love alone distinguishes good actions from evil ones. Thus love makes one person fierce, while wickedness makes another charmingly gentle. A father may spank a son, and a child molester may caress him. If you offered a choice between being struck and being caressed, who would not prefer to be caressed rather than struck? Yet if you look at the intentions in these two cases, it is love that strikes and wickedness that caresses. Our actions must be judged by whether they are rooted in love. For many actions appear to be good, but they are not rooted in love. Thorns also have flowers. Here is the rule: Love, and do what you want.

Love Is the Distinguishing Mark of the True Christian

Beloved, let us love one another; for love is of God, and he who loves is born of God and knows God. He who does not love does not know God; for God is love.

1 JOHN 4:7-8

MORNING READING

Love alone distinguishes between the children of God and the children of the devil. They may all sign themselves with the sign of the cross of Christ; they may all respond "Amen" to prayers and sing "Alleluia"; they may all be baptized, and come to church, and even build the church themselves. But we can discern the children of God from the children of the devil by their love alone. Those who have love are born of God; those who have no love are not born of God. This is the great sign, the great distinction. Possess whatever you want, but if you are lacking this one thing, the rest will be of no value to you.

We are born to love, we live to love, and we will die to love still more.

ST. JOSEPH CAFASSO

FOR REFLECTION

Jesus, in which unlovable person in my life are you waiting for me to love you?

EVENING READING

Love is the pearl of great price that the merchant in the Gospel was seeking [see Mt 13:46]. Without it, nothing else you may possess will do you any good. And if love is all you have, it will be enough for you. For now, you are looking to God by faith, but then, you will actually see the One you have been looking for. For if we can love him even now when we cannot see him, how we will embrace him in love when we finally can see him! But how are we trained to love? By loving our brothers. You may say to me, "I have not seen God"; but can you say to me, "I have not seen my brother or sister"? Love them. For if you love the brother you can see, at the same time you will see God as well, because you will see love itself, and that is where God dwells.

We Must Love Others for the Saints They May Become

And you, who once were estranged and hostile in mind, doing evil deeds, he has now reconciled in his body of flesh by his death, in order to present you holy and blameless and irreproachable before him.

COLOSSIANS 1:21-22

MORNING READING

You do not love in your enemies what they are, but what you would have them to become. Suppose there is a log of timber lying around. A skilled carpenter sees the log, not yet planed, just as it was hewn in the forest. He takes a liking to it because he wants to make something out of it. He is not attracted to it for the purpose of leaving it as it is. In his craft he has seen what it will become, and his liking is for what he will make of it, not for what it is now. In the same way we say that God loved sinners. Did he love us sinners for the purpose of keeping us sinners? Our Carpenter viewed us as unplaned logs, and he had in mind the building he would make of us, not the rough timber that we were.

If God causes you to suffer much, it is a sign that he has great designs for you, and that he certainly intends to make you a saint.

ST. IGNATIUS LOYOLA

FOR REFLECTION

Father, help me to see my enemies as you see them—and as you see they could one day be.

EVENING READING

As the Lord viewed you, you too must view your enemies, those who oppose you, raging, biting with words, frustrating you with their slander, harassing you with their hatred. You must remember that they are human beings; you must see all their actions against you as merely human works, while they themselves are the works of God. That your enemies have been created is God's doing; that they hate you and wish your ruin is their own doing. What should you say about them in your mind? "Lord, be merciful to them, forgive them their sins, put the fear of God in them, change them!" You are loving in them not what they are, but what you would have them to become.

We Must Love Our Enemies
As a Physician Loves a Patient

Jesus said, "Father, forgive them; for they know not what they do."
LUKE 23:34

MORNING READING

Do not be slow to love your enemies. Are there those who rage against you? If so, pray for them. Do they hate you? Pity them. It is actually the sick fever in their souls that hates you; one day they will be healed, and they will thank you. Be like our physicians: How do they love those who are ill? Is it the illness itself that they love? If they loved their patients for being sick, they would want them always to be sick. But they love those who are ill, not so that they will remain that way, but so that their illness will be healed. And how much does the doctor put up with when patients are delirious! What rude, foul language! Often such patients go so far as to strike the doctor. Yet the doctor attacks the fever while forgiving the patient.

Let us learn to feel for the ills our neighbors suffer, and we will learn to endure the ills they inflict.
ST. JOHN CHRYSOSTOM

FOR REFLECTION
Great Physician, give me a physician's heart.

EVENING READING
What shall we say, brothers and sisters: Does the physician love his enemy? No—he hates his enemy, because his enemy is the disease, not the patient. Even if a delirious patient strikes him, he still loves the patient but hates the fever that causes the delirium. For who is it that really struck him? Not the patient, but the delirium, the fever, the illness itself. So he works to get rid of the sickness that fights against him, so that the patient who survives will give him thanks. And so should you. If your enemies hate you, and hate you without cause, remember that the ungodly passions of the world control them like a fever, making them hate you.

DAY 47
Do Our Actions Contradict Our Words of Love for Christ?

Little children, let us not love in word or speech but in deed and in truth.

1 JOHN 3:18

MORNING READING

"Whoever denies that Jesus is the Christ," that same person "is an anti-Christ" [see 1 Jn 2:22]. So then let us find out who denies this—but we must look at actions rather than words. For if we ask the question, all who are Christians reply with one voice that Jesus is the Christ. But let their voices be silent for a little while so we can question their lives. If Scripture itself tells us that denial is possible not only by words, but by actions as well, then certainly we find many antichrists who profess Christ with their mouths but dissent from him by their way of life. Where do we find this in Scripture? "For they confess that they know God, but in their deeds they deny him" [see Ti 1:16].

If a man has words but no works, he is like a tree with leaves but no fruit. Just as a tree laden with fruit is also leafy, the man of good works will also have good words.

THE SAYINGS OF THE FATHERS

FOR REFLECTION

Through what actions have I betrayed my words and denied you today, Lord?

EVENING READING

Whoever denies Christ in his actions is an antichrist. Instead of listening to what he says, I look at the life he leads. When actions speak loudly, who needs words? For what evil man does not wish to speak well? What does our Lord say to people like this? "You hypocrites—how can you speak good things when you are evil?" [see Mt 12:34]. Your voices may ring in my ears, he tells them, but I look into your thoughts. I see an evil will there, and you are only making a show of your false fruits. I know what I must gather and where to find it. I do not gather "figs from thistles" or "grapes from thorns"; for "every tree is known by its fruit" [see Mt 7:16]. The worst liar is the antichrist who with his mouth professes that Jesus is the Christ, but by his actions denies him.

Real Love Must Sometimes Be Tough

Better is open rebuke than hidden love. Faithful are the wounds of a friend; profuse are the kisses of an enemy.

PROVERBS 27:5-6

MORNING READING

If you want to preserve love, brothers and sisters, above all do not imagine it to be something resigned and apathetic. Nor is love preserved by the kind of weakness and laziness that masquerades as meekness. These attitudes are not loving at all. Do not imagine that you love your children when you never discipline them, or that you love your neighbors when you never admonish them. This is not love, but mere weakness. Let your love be eager to correct, to reform. If there is good behavior, let it please you; but if there is bad behavior, let it be reproved and corrected. Do not love the error, but the person who commits the error. When you love the person, you take away the error; when you esteem the person, you correct the fault.

Eating and drinking do not make friendships—such friendship even robbers and murderers have. But if we are friends, if we truly care for one another, let us help one another spiritually.... Let us hinder those things that lead our friends away to hell.

ST. JOHN CHRYSOSTOM

FOR REFLECTION

Lord, give me wisdom to find the right words when someone I love needs correction.

EVENING READING

Sometimes hatred is charming, while love must show itself severe. Some people, for example, may hate their enemies, yet pretend to be their friends. They praise them when they see them doing wrong, because they want them to be ruined; they want them to plunge headfirst and blindly over the precipice of their lusts, perhaps never to return. They smear them over with flattery—and in this way, they hate even as they praise. Yet others, when they see their friends doing something similar, will call them back. And if their friends will not listen, they will resort if they must to stinging rebukes, scolding and quarrels. Do you see how hatred may show itself sweetly pleasing while love quarrels?

DAY 49
Those We Love in God Will Never Be Lost

Man's days are like those of grass; like a flower of the field he blooms; the wind sweeps over him and he is gone, and his place knows him no more. But the kindness of the Lord is from eternity to eternity toward those who fear him.

PSALM 103:15-17, NAB

MORNING READING

I had acquired a very dear friend, from our association in our studies. But he was not then truly my friend, nor did he ever become truly my friend, for there is no true friendship except between those whom you bind together, Lord, and who cling to you by that love "poured into our hearts through the Holy Spirit" [see Rom 5:5]. If your delight is in souls, my friends, let them be loved in God, for they too are changeable, and they will perish and pass away if they are not firmly established in him. In him, then, let them be loved; and draw to him along with you as many souls as you can. Say to them: "He is the One we should love. He is the One. He has created the world, and he is not far from us. For when he created the world, he did not abandon it. All that exists comes from him and is in him."

If the bond of your communion is love, devotion and Christian perfection, then your friendship will be precious indeed: precious because it has its origin in God, because it is maintained in God, and because it will endure forever in him.

ST. FRANCIS DE SALES

FOR REFLECTION

Let those of my friends who do not know you, Jesus, encounter you through me.

EVENING READING

What madness to love another man as if he were something more than a mere mortal! I had poured out my soul onto the dust by loving one who must die as if he would never die. Yes, we mourn when a friend dies—the gloom of sorrow, the steeping of the heart in tears, all sweetness turned into bitterness—and when the life of the dying is lost, we who remain alive feel dead. Yet blessed are those who love you, Lord, and their friends in you. For they are the only ones who will never lose anyone dear to them, since all who are dear to them are in You, our God, who can never be lost.

"This Healthy Lesson ..."

*God Works in an Evil World
Through Us*

Do Not Despair Because of the World's Wickedness

Do all things without grumbling or questioning, that you may be blameless and innocent, children of God without blemish in the midst of a crooked and perverse generation, among whom you shine as lights in the world, holding fast the word of life.

PHILIPPIANS 2:14-16

MORNING READING

Pray as much as you are able. Evils abound, and God has willed that, for now, evils abound. Would that evil people did not abound, and then evils would not abound! "These are bad times," people are saying, "troublesome times!" If only our lives were all good, our times would be good, for we ourselves make our times—as we are, so are our times. But what can we do? After all, we cannot convert the mass of humanity to a good life. But let the few who do listen to the will of God live good lives; and let the few who live good lives endure the many who do not. The good are the wheat, still on the threshing floor; and though the chaff lies with them here, the chaff will not come with them to the barn.

Truly, matters in the world are in a bad state; but if you and I begin in earnest to reform ourselves, a really good beginning will have been made.

ST. PETER OF ALCANTARA

FOR REFLECTION

Lord, make us salt, light, and leaven in the world.

EVENING READING

Why are we sad; why do we blame God? Evils abound in the world so that the world will fail to seduce us into loving it. Those who have despised the world with all its attractions were great men and women, faithful saints; yet we find it hard to despise the world, even as disfigured as it is. The world is evil; yes, it is evil; and yet it is loved as if it were good. What makes it evil? There is much in the world that is good: For the heavens and the earth and the sea, and the things that are in all these—the fish, the birds, the trees—are not evil. All these are good, but evil people make the world evil. Yet since we cannot be without evil people, while we live in the world we must pour out our sighs to the Lord our God, and endure the evils, so that we may attain to the things that are good.

God Allows the Wicked to Prosper to Remind Us of the Temporary Value of Worldly Riches

I was envious of the arrogant when I saw them prosper though they were wicked.... Though I tried to understand this it seemed to me too difficult, till I entered the sanctuary of God and considered their final destiny.

PSALM 73:3, 16, 17, NAB

MORNING READING

In this present time we must learn to take in stride the ills to which even good people are subject, and to view as cheap the kinds of worldly blessings that even the wicked enjoy. Consequently, even in those situations of life where the justice of God is not apparent, He offers us this healthy lesson. For we do not know by what judgment of God this good person is poor and that bad one rich; why the one who, in our opinion, should suffer severely for a life of abandon nevertheless enjoys so many pleasures—while sorrows pursue the one whose praiseworthy life seems to merit happiness; why the innocent may leave the court without justice and even condemned, while the guilty adversary leaves court unpunished, why the ungodly enjoys good health, while the godly languishes in sickness, why criminals are crowned with honors, while the blameless are buried, unmourned.

Let us not esteem worldly prosperity or adversity as things real or of any moment, but let us live elsewhere and raise all our attention to heaven; esteeming sin as the only true evil, and nothing truly good but virtue that unites us to God.

ST. GREGORY NAZIANZEN

FOR REFLECTION

When life seems unfair, Lord, teach me to value the precious gifts from you that mere circumstances can neither steal nor bestow.

EVENING READING

So even though we do not know by what judgment these things are done or permitted to be done by God yet it is healthy for us to learn to view as cheap such things, whether good or evil, that attach indiscriminantly to good people and bad, so that we desire instead those good things that belong only to good people, and flee those bad things that belong only to evil people. But when we will have come to Judgment Day, we will then recognize the justice of all God's judgments.

DAY 52

Unjust Governments Rob the People, But Just Governments Bless Them

First of all, then, I urge that supplications, prayers, intercessions, and thanksgivings be made for all men, for kings and all who are in high positions, that we may lead a quiet and peaceable life, godly and respectful in every way.

1 TIMOTHY 2:1-2

MORNING READING

If justice is taken away, then, what are kingdoms but great robberies? For what are robberies themselves, but little kingdoms? Like a kingdom, the robbers' band is made of human beings, ruled by the authority of a leader, knit together by a pact of confederacy; and the booty is divided by the law they have agreed upon. If, by the admittance of more outlaws into the band, this evil increases to such a degree that it seizes territories, establishes a capital, takes possession of cities, and subdues peoples, it takes on the explicit title of "kingdom," for that is now clearly what it has become. But this is not because the robbers are any less greedy. It is simply because the law now gives sanction to their greed.

The world would have peace if only the men of politics would follow the Gospels.

ST. BIRGITTA OF SWEDEN

FOR REFLECTION

Lord God of the nations, give us rulers who love you, love justice, and love peace.

EVENING READING

Rulers are happy if they rule justly: if they are not made arrogant by flattery, if they make their power the servant of God's majesty, if they fear, love and worship God; if, more than their own kingdom, they love that heavenly kingdom in which they are not afraid to share their glory; if they are slow to punish, ready to pardon; if they use their power only as is necessary for government and the defense of the republic, and not for personal vendettas; if they grant pardon, not that crime may go unpunished, but with the hope that criminals may reform, if they would rather rule over their own unruly passions than over a nation; and if they do all these things, not from an eager desire for empty glory, but through love of eternal happiness with God.

Love Begins in Sharing
What We Have With Others

Tell the rich ... to do good, to be rich in good works, to be generous, ready to share, thus accumulating as treasure a good foundation for the future, so as to win the life that is true life.

1 TIMOTHY 6:17-18, NAB

MORNING READING

"If anyone has the world's goods and sees his brother hungry, yet closes his heart against him, how can the love of God be living in him?" [see 1 Jn 3:17]. See now where love begins. If you are not yet capable of laying down your life for your brother, you are at least capable of giving him some of your goods. Even now let love stir your heart, not to act so that others will praise you, but to act out of a rich depth of mercy, thinking only of the one in need. For if you cannot even give out of your abundance to someone in need, how could you possibly lay down your life for anyone?

Of what use are riches in eternity?

ST. ALOYSIUS GONZAGA

FOR REFLECTION

Remind me daily, Jesus, that whatever I do for one of your children, I do for you.

EVENING READING

There sits your money in your purse, which thieves may take from you. And even if thieves do not take it, when you die you will leave it behind—provided that you have not already lost it by then. What will you do with it? Your brother is hungry, he is in need—perhaps he is anxious, pressed by creditors. He is your brother; you have both been bought; the same price was paid for both of you: You were both redeemed by the blood of Christ. See now if you have compassion, you who have the world's goods. Perhaps you say, "How does this concern me? Am I to spend my money to keep him out of trouble?" If this is the answer your heart gives you, then the love of the Father does not live in you. And if the love of the Father does not live in you, then you are not born of God. How can you claim to be a Christian? You have the name but not the deeds.

Sowing Good Works Reaps a Harvest of Joy

He who sows virtue has a sure reward.

PROVERBS 11:18, NAB

MORNING READING

"Those who sow in tears shall reap in joy" [see Ps 126:5]. What shall we sow? Good deeds. Works of mercy are our seeds. Why do you long for some great field where you could sow plentifully? There is no wider field you can sow than Christ, who has willed that we sow in himself. Your soil is the Church; sow as much as you can. But, you say, you do not have enough money to do this. Well, then, do you have the good will to do it? If you do not have a good will, then no matter what you sow, it will amount to nothing. But in the same way, you should not despair if you think you have nothing to sow, as long as you have a good will. For what do you sow? Mercy. And what will you reap? Peace. Did the angels say, "Peace on earth to rich men"? No—they said, "Peace on earth to men of good will" [see Lk 2:14].

The bread you store up belongs to the hungry; the cloak that lies in your chest belongs to the naked; the gold that you have hidden in the ground belongs to the poor.

ST. BASIL

FOR REFLECTION

Lord, what do I have today that I could sow into the rich field of those around me?

EVENING READING

Even beggars who must spend their time asking for alms have something to bestow on one another in times of trouble. God has not forsaken them in this regard, for they too have something by which their willingness to give alms can be tested. This man cannot walk; so the one who is able to walk can lend his feet to the lame. The one who sees can lend his eyes to the blind; and the one who is young and healthy can lend his strength to the old or the disabled by carrying him: When the one is poor, the other is rich.

"The Cry of the Heart …"

Our Prayer and God's Response

DAY 55

God Does Not Always Answer Prayer
As We Expect

For the eyes of the Lord are upon the righteous, and his ears are open to their prayer. But the face of the Lord is against those that do evil.

1 PETER 3:12

MORNING READING

We must distinguish God's different ways of hearing prayer. For we find some who are not given what they want, but rather what will contribute to their salvation. On the other hand, we find some whose wishes are granted, but it is not for their good. God showed St. Paul what it means to have a prayer answered for our good: "My grace is sufficient for you, for strength is perfected in weakness" [see 2 Cor 12:9]. God told him, "You have sought me, have cried, have called out to me three times, and I heard your cry; I did not turn away from you. But I know what I have to do. You would have me take away the medicine that stings you, yet I know the sickness that burdens you."

If we remember the words of the Apostle Paul that "we do not know what we ought to pray for" [see Rom 8:26], we will see that we sometimes ask for things opposed to our salvation, and that we are most providentially refused our requests by the One who sees what is good for us with greater rightness and truth than we can.

ABBOT ISAAC

FOR REFLECTION

Father, grant me what I need rather than what I want, ai
near me when my prayer is answered.

EVENING READING

Do we think we can find some wicked, impious person who was
heard according to his wishes rather than his good? Yes: the devil
himself. He asked God to allow him power over Job, and he
received what he asked for. So the devil asked for a holy man, to
tempt him, and his wish was granted; while the Apostle Paul asked
that the thorn in his flesh might be taken from him, and his wish
was not granted. But it was still the apostle rather than the devil
whom God heard. For the apostle was heard, not according to his
wishes, but for his salvation; and the devil was heard, according to
his wishes, but for his damnation. For Job was turned over to the
devil to be tempted so that, by standing the test, he would be a
torment to the devil.

The Great Physician May Deny a Request for Our Spiritual Health

"Behold, happy is the man whom God reproves; therefore despise not the chastening of the Almighty. For he wounds, but he binds up; he smites, but his hands heal."

Job 5:17-18

MORNING READING

We must understand, then, that even though God does not always give us what we want, he gives us what we need for our salvation. Suppose you ask a physician for something that would be harmful, and he knows it would be harmful; what should he do? Let's say that you ask for a drink of cold water. If it would do you good, and he gives it to you right away, then surely you cannot say that he has not heard you. On the other hand, if it would do you harm, and so he does not give it to you, you still cannot say that he has not heard you, just because he contradicted your will. Instead, he has heard you for the sake of your health.

God hands over the body and soul to weakness in order to purify them in contempt of earthly things and in the love of his majesty. He wounds and he heals them; he crucifies them on his cross in order to glorify them in his glory; in short, he gives them death in order to have them live in eternity.

ST. VINCENT DE PAUL

FOR REFLECTION

Loving Doctor of my soul, give me the medicine I need—with a
spoonful of your sweet grace to help it go down.

EVENING READING

So learn to pray to God in such a way that you are trusting him as
your Physician to do what he knows is best. Confess to him the
disease, and let him choose the remedy. Then hold tight to love,
for what he does will cut and sting you. You may cry out, and
your cries may not stop the cutting, the burning, and the pain; yet
he knows how deep the festering flesh lies. While you want him to
take his hands off you, he considers only the extent of the
infection; he knows how far he must go. He is not listening to you
according to what you want, but according to what will heal you.

When We Long for God, Our Longing Becomes a Perpetual Prayer

As the hind longs for the running waters, so my soul longs for you, O God. Athirst is my soul for God, the living God. When shall I go and behold the face of God?

PSALM 42:2-3, NAB

MORNING READING

Let your desire be before God, and "the Father, who sees in secret, will reward you" [see Mt 6:6]. It is your heart's desire that is your prayer; and if your desire continues without interruption, your prayer continues as well. For it was not without meaning that the Apostle Paul said, "Pray without ceasing" [see 1 Th 5:17]. Are we to "pray without ceasing" in the sense of kneeling, prostrating ourselves, or lifting our hands? For if he speaks of prayer in this sense, I believe we cannot do it "without ceasing." Yet there is another inward kind of prayer without ceasing that is the desire of the heart. Whatever else you are doing, if you are also longing for that eternal Sabbath rest with God, you are not ceasing to pray.

For me, prayer means launching out of the heart toward God; a cry of grateful love from the crest of joy or the trough of despair: it is a vast, supernatural force that opens out my heart, and binds me close to Jesus.

St. Thérèse of Lisieux

FOR REFLECTION

Jesus, let my longing heart never cease to offer up the perpetual prayer of my desire to be united to you.

EVENING READING

If you want to pray without ceasing, never cease to long for God. The continuation of your longing is the continuation of your prayer; and if you cease to long for him, this prayer will also cease. Who are those, then, who have ceased to utter this prayer? Those of whom it was said, "Because iniquity will abound, the love of many will grow cold" [see Mt 24:12]. The freezing of love is the silence of the heart; the flame of love is the cry of the heart. If love still continues, you are still lifting up your voice; if you are always lifting up your voice, you are always longing for something; and if you are always longing for something yet to come, you are calling to mind the eternal Sabbath rest that God has promised.

DAY 58

Our Souls Must Be Stretched
by a Holy Desire for God

We know that when he appears we shall be like him, for we shall see him as he is. And every one who thus hopes in him purifies himself as he is pure.

1 JOHN 3:2-3

MORNING READING

The whole life of a good Christian is a holy desire to see God as he is. Now what you long for, you do not yet see, but longing makes you capable of being filled when at last you behold what you have desired. It is just as if you want to put something in a pouch, and knowing how large is the thing you want to put in it, you stretch the opening of the pouch. As it was, the pouch was too small to contain what you have for it. In the same way God, by making us wait in hope, stretches our desire; by making us desire, he stretches our soul; by stretching our soul, he makes it capable of holding more. So let us desire, brothers, for we shall be filled.

Lord our God, grant us grace to desire you with our whole heart, that so desiring, we may seek and find you; and so finding you, we may love you; and loving you, we may hate those sins from which you have redeemed us.

ST. ANSELM OF CANTERBURY

FOR REFLECTION

Stretch me, God; open me wide to be filled so full that nothing but you can find a place inside me.

EVENING READING

This is our life as Christians: to be filled with longing. But holy desire fills us only to the extent that we cut off our longings from the love of the world. You must first empty what you want to be filled. If you are to be filled with what is good, then you must pour out what is evil. Suppose that God wants to fill you with honey: If you are filled with vinegar, where will you put the honey? Whatever was put into the container must be poured out again, and the container itself must be cleaned with hard scrubbing, so that it will be ready for whatever is to be put in it, whatever that may be: gold or honey or wine. In truth, we are to be filled with Something beyond words: God himself. We must stretch ourselves out to him, then, so that when he comes, he may fill us.

Our Longing for God
Brings Us Closer to Heaven

And I saw the holy city, new Jerusalem, coming down out of heaven from God, prepared as a bride adorned for her husband; and I heard a loud voice from the throne saying, "Behold, the dwelling of God is with men. He will dwell with them, and they shall be his people."

REVELATION 21:2-3

MORNING READING

That chaste city of yours, Lord, our mother that is above, that is free! Holding fast to you with sublime love, it shines and glows with your light like a perpetual noon. House, full of light and splendor! I have loved your beauty, and the place of the habitation of the glory of my Lord, your builder and owner. Let my wanderings sigh after you, and I will ask of him who made you that he would possess me in you, for he is my Maker as well. I have gone astray, like a lost sheep; yet upon the shoulders of my Shepherd, your builder, I hope that I may be brought back to you.

I have been made for heaven, and heaven for me.

ST. JOSEPH CAFASSO

FOR REFLECTION

Father, sing me a song of the eternal homeland that I have never seen; keep alive in me a homesickness for heaven, an aching for the dwelling place where I will see you at last, face to face.

EVENING READING

I will sing to you, Lord, songs of love—groaning with groanings that are for now unutterable in my pilgrimage, and remembering Jerusalem, with my heart raised up toward it, Jerusalem my country, Jerusalem my mother, and you yourself, Lord, the Ruler over it, the Enlightener, the Father, the Guardian, the Husband, the chaste and strong Delight, the solid Joy, the Source of all things good beyond description! You are all these things at once, because you are the one supreme and true Good. And I will not be turned away until the time when you gather together all that I am from this present scattering, this deformity, into the peace of that dearest mother, Jerusalem—where the first fruits of my spirit are found, and from which come all these things that are promised me. I will not be turned away until you have conformed me and confirmed me there forever, my God, my fount of mercy.

When This World Passes Away, We Will Find Our Eternal Sabbath in God

So then, there remains a sabbath rest for the people of God; for whoever enters God's rest also ceases from his labors as God did from his. Let us therefore strive to enter that rest.

HEBREWS 4:9-11

MORNING READING

Grant us, Lord God, your peace: for you have supplied us with all things. Give us the peace of quietness, the peace of the Sabbath, the peace without an evening to end it. For all this most beautiful order of things in your creation, all so very good, must nevertheless pass away, their courses being finished—for you made them to have a morning and evening. But the seventh day, the day of our final rest, is without any evening, nor does the sun ever set on it—for you have sanctified it to last forever. After all the works of your creation, which were very good, on the seventh day you rested, even though your own eternal rest was unbroken by the act of creation.

I am a prisoner too—with all this wide and beautiful creation before me, the restless soul longs to enjoy its liberty and rest beyond its bound. When the Father calls his child, how readily will he be obeyed!

ST. ELIZABETH ANN SETON

FOR REFLECTION

May I never seek rest, my Lord, my God, until I find my rest in you, and you find your rest in me.

EVENING READING

The voice of your Book tells us about your resting on the Sabbath so that we may read ahead of time how after our own works are done—which are also very good, because you have given them to us to do—we too shall repose in you in the Sabbath of eternal life. For even then, you shall rest in us even as you now work in us. And thus shall our rest be yours, even as the works we do now are your works accomplished through us. But you, Lord, are always working and always at rest. You are goodness itself, you need no good other than yourself, and you are forever at rest, because you yourself are rest.

NOTES

INTRODUCTION

1. *The Confessions*, (IV.4, 12)
2. *The Confessions*, (I.1)

READINGS

1. *The Confessions* (I.1; VI.16)
2. *The Confessions* (I. 4)
3. *The Confessions* (X.22-23); *Exposition on Psalm 85:6*
4. *The Confessions* (XIII.9; X.1)
5. *The Confessions* (II.5; IV.12)
6. *The Confessions* (X.28; X.1-2)
7. *The Confessions* (IV.12)
8. *Second Homily on the First Letter of St. John* (10)
9. *Sermons on New Testament Lessons* (XXVII.11); *The Confessions* (VII.18)
10. *The Confessions* (X.43)
11. *Tenth Homily on the First Letter of St. John* (5, 6)
12. *The Confessions* (XI.4; X.34)
13. *Second Homily on the First Letter of St. John* (11)
14. *The Confessions* (IV.11)
15. *The Confessions* (II.6)
16. *The Confessions* (VIII.11)
17. *Tenth Homily on the First Letter of St. John* (4)
18. *The Confessions* (X.42); *Second Homily on the First Letter of St. John* (13)
19. *The Confessions* (VIII.5)
20. *Homily 36 on the Gospel of St. John* (4); *Sermon 59 on the Gospels* (1, 2)
21. *The Confessions* (II.1; VII.7-8)
22. *The Confessions* (V.2); *Sixth Homily on the First Letter of St. John* (3)
23. *Fourth Homily on the First Letter of St. John* (10); *Fourth Homily on the Second Letter of St. John* (11)
24. *Homilies on New Testament Lessons* (VIII.8)
25. *Ninth Homily on the First Letter of St. John* (4)
26. *Ninth Homily on the First Letter of St. John* (5, 6)
27. *The Confessions* (IV.1; V.1)
28. *The Confessions* (X.1, 2, 3)
29. *The Confessions* (X.39, 32)

30. *The Confessions* (X.28, 29)
31. *The Confessions* (VIII.5)
32. *Fourth Homily on the First Letter of St. John* (3)
33. *Third Homily on the First Letter of St. John* (11, 12)
34. *The Confessions* (X.31)
35. *The Confessions* (X.38); *Eighth Homily on the First Letter of St. John* (2)
36. *The Confessions* (X.23)
37. *The Confessions* (XII.10; XI.2)
38. *The Confessions* (VI.5; XIII.23)
39. *The Confessions* (VI.5; XII.14; XIII.15)
40. *The Confessions* (XI.2)
41. *Third Homily on the First Letter of St. John* (13)
42. *Third Homily on the First Letter of St. John* (1); *Fifth Homily on the First Letter of St. John* (6)
43. *Sixth Homily on the First Letter of St. John* (7, 8)
44. *Fifth Homily on the First Letter of St. John* (7)
45. *Eighth Homily on the First Letter of St. John* (10)
46. *Eighth Homily on the First Letter of St. John* (11)
47. *Second Homily on the First Letter of St. John* (8); *Third Homily on the First Letter of St. John* (8)
48. *Seventh Homily on the First Letter of St. John* (11); *Tenth Homily on the First Letter of St. John* (7)
49. *The Confessions* (IV.4, 12, 7, 8, 9)
50. *Homilies on New Testament Lessons* (XXX.7)
51. *City of God* (XX.2)
52. *City of God* (IV.4; V.24)
53. *Fifth Homily on the First Letter of St. John* (12)
54. *Exposition on Psalm 126:5*
55. *Sixth Homily on the First Letter of St. John* (7)
56. *Sixth Homily on the First Letter of St. John* (8)
57. *Homilies on Psalms 38, 13*
58. *Fourth Homily on the First Letter of St. John* (6)
59. *The Confessions* (XII.15, 16)
60. *The Confessions* (XIII.35, 36, 37)

Breakfast With the Saints
120 Readings from Great Christians

What do the saints have to say about things that matter to you—
passion, feelings, friendship, healing, money, prayer? Why not ask
them yourself in *Breakfast with the Saints?*

Do you have trouble getting up in the morning? Check in with
St. Patrick on waking up. Do you sometimes put your foot in
your mouth? Blessed Humbert has some good advice on thinking
before speaking. Are you concerned for the earth's environment?
Join St. Francis of Assisi's praise for all creation.

These 120 selections from or about the saints offer you fresh,
thought-provoking perspectives on the real issues of life. And they
introduce you to spiritual heroes who set an example of virtuous
living. Hardcover, 160 pp., $14.99